MAD DADDY

Myers, Mintz and the Moondog and How Cleveland, Ohio, Changed Rock Radio

By Janice and Mike Olszewski
Foreword by Johnny Holliday

BearManorMedia.com

This book is dedicated to everyone who keeps the
true spirit of radio alive.

Table of Contents

THE MAD DADDY I KNEW
Foreword

By Johnny Holliday

Pete Myers. Yeah, I knew Pete Myers. Probably as well as anyone other than his family, and that's because I worked with him at two different stations. First, at WHK in Cleveland and later on at New York's WINS. I was only 21 years old when I arrived at Cleveland's 1420 and even though I'd been at a couple of stations it was still early in my career. Radio was going through its transition losing audience to TV and we were part of that first generation of entertainers called "disc jockeys". What a time it was! There were still plenty of listeners, but in towns across the U.S. that audience was getting younger and younger, many of them my age, and we all knew radio was heading in an exciting new direction.

It wasn't just the music, but the folks who brought it to the public, and we were all part of a very small fraternity. By 1959 a lot of the music on the charts wasn't even close to those early rebellious days of rock and roll, and you could make a pretty strong argument that the DJ's were generating the excitement. Even then, disc jockeys were like nomads. You went where the work was and shared a studio with a lot of different people. You cut your teeth at small stations, honed your craft and when you were ready went to the big cities. That's how I met Pete Myers.

There were big names back then and we all learned from each other. Reputations carried, too. You had Porky Chedwick out of Pittsburgh, Dick Clark was in Philadelphia where a guy named Hy Lit was getting some attention with Chicago's Dick Biondi and "Murray the K" Kaufman and "Cousin Brucie" Morrow in New York standing in the wings ready to pounce. Of course, everyone knew about Alan Freed who had left Cleveland years before I arrived in 1958. It's an old cliché but it rings true. It was a different time and a different place, and the city on the shores of Lake Erie was a whole new world for this "refugee from the Sunshine State". It was a major city with major radio talent, and two Bills…Gordon and Randle… who seemed to own the airwaves.

Bill Gordon came from WHBQ / Memphis, the same station where a guy he hired… Dewey Phillips… was holding court. Gordon did some time at WHK along with some other stations and even TV. They called him "Smoochie" because of his sign off, "Stay smoochie you rascal, you!" Gordon was a different kind of radio personality. He talked over records, sometimes using the latest hits for music beds, and his audience loved what he had to say. Then there was Bill Randle…

Cool, confident and determined, Randle helped make stars out of Elvis Presley and Johnnie Ray, among others, and he was happy to let you know it, too. Still, this guy had an undeniable ear for hits, and when I got to WHK he was about to break another act on WERE. Ready for it? The Mormon Tabernacle Choir and "The Battle Hymn of the Republic". That was the power of Bill Randle. Don't get me wrong. There was a lot of competition on the radio dial then, but WHK had its "big guns", too. Pete Myers would be one of them.

When I started there, WHK had gone through a "purge". There were two guys left from the old staff and they were Myers and Tom Brown. Myers cut an impressive figure. A pleasant looking guy, with a casual smile and you noticed that he was so nattily dressed. He was soft spoken off the air, and…being a few years older with a bit more radio time under his belt…always there with some sage advice for an up-and-coming jock. You learn by watching and listening, and radio at that time and place was a great classroom!

Your show was an extension of you, a reflection of your personality, and if you're having fun chances are the audience is, too. "Lovable, laughable" Pete Myers was that kind of guy. It was a safe haven, your escape from the problems of daily life, and plenty of music to boot. It was a far cry from the guy who hosted that crazy show later in the evening…. the Mad Daddy!

We'd heard about Myers' "alter ego", the parachute jump, the "zoomerating" and all the rest. Could this be the same guy? I remember listening to his show almost in disbelief. We'd had numerous conversations, but his being such a private guy I don't remember any of those exchanges being more than five minutes tops! The Mad Daddy was a tsunami of words heading toward you at a hundred miles an hour with the occasional cackle thrown in before those crazy rhythm and blues tunes that didn't seem to show upon the weekly Tunedex. What would he play next, and what would he say? Was this guy for real? I had to see him in action!

The jocks had just done an appearance, I think it was a charity basketball game with our team the WHK Radio One-Ders playing a high school faculty, and Mad Daddy was on my car radio. Instead of heading home I drove to the station to get a look. Turns out that wasn't as easy as I thought. Big cities had pretty strict rules about unions, and engineers spun the records and worked the equipment. Myers' producer saw me and asked," What are you doing here?" Myers made personal appearances as Mad Daddy, but the guy working the show said it was a two-man operation and no one but him was allowed in the studio. I kind of got that hint when I saw the studio window covered with newspapers. Even so, I had a chance to get a quick peek and couldn't believe what I saw.

He treated the studio like his stage, even wearing his Mad Daddy cape to help him get in character. Cloth swirling every which way, he was loud and brash and high energy but one thing he was not. The guy behind the mic had told Pete Myers to sit in the far corner of his mind to make way for his other side, the lyrical lunatic spreading his own brand of radio bedlam to an audience that could never get enough. The Mad Daddy was in total control in the studio with his quirky choreography and peculiar poetry and couldn't be distracted in even the slightest way. Wow!

We both made it to New York City, and I'll take the opportunity to clear up what might be considered an urban legend. Was Pete Myers a failure in the Big Apple? Not in my book. That audience may not have embraced the Mad Daddy the way the folks did back in Ohio but consider this. Myers had made it to the most important radio market in the world. Competitive, too. He was on a 50-thousand-watt station that took his "lovable, laughable" personality well beyond the boundaries of New York state. He rose to a level of success that most broadcasters, especially at that time, could only dream of and was there for close to a decade. Even so, Pete Myers obviously wanted more for himself and the audience.

The authors, Janice and Mike, also give us a look at the mood of the radio industry and the times in general, and compare the paths taken by other players in this story. Alan Freed made some poor decisions possibly linked to his own arrogance or ego and paid dearly as a result. Then there's Leo Mintz, a very bright guy and successful businessman, the owner of Record Rendezvous. Mintz bought a lot of radio ad time and, as a result, moved a lot of product but he also saw trends and made his downtown store the pop culture hub of Northeast Ohio. Quincy Jones and Berry Gordy knew that location well and even today can tell you the path they took from the city's Union Terminal Train Station to Mintz' Prospect Avenue store. There were plenty of other record stores. There was Tommy Edwards "Hillbilly Heaven" on the city's near west side, the new suburban shopping centers like Southgate had "Bandstand" and every department store had racks and racks of records. But Record Rendezvous was the place to see stars like Tommy Sands, Vic Damone and so many more, meeting hundreds of fans and spreading the word nationwide it was "the" place to be in Cleveland. Mintz also had a keen sense for recognizing distinctive trends and radio voices and showed them how to capitalize on their talents. In the end, Leo Mintz likely had the only story with a happy ending.

Still, this is mainly a tale about the life, times and legend of a guy who called himself the Mad Daddy. I can't tell you how much I admired his talent and friendship, and his passing affected me deeply. I also truly believe that if he were alive today Mad Daddy would own the nighttime airwaves no matter where he worked. He was funny, brilliant, energetic, driven, focused, enthusiastic, dramatic, unpredictable, highly creative, observant, insightful, determined, charismatic, dedicated and so very much more. You bet I knew Pete Myers. Now it's your turn, and you begin by turning the page.

Johnny Holliday
Summer 2023

Acknowledgements

In 1985, I was working at WERE / Cleveland, and I presented a series of reports about the rich history of the Northeast Ohio radio scene. It caught the attention of local businessman and entrepreneur Larry Collins, who introduced me to Pete "Mad Daddy" Myers when he dropped off a reel of rare recordings. That tape changed my life as I researched this amazing character and even pursued a graduate degree basing my masters' thesis on Daddy's legacy. Janice's and my life were changed for the better and special thanks go to Larry Collins. This part of Pete "Mad Daddy" Myers' history would not have been completed, or even started, without his valuable input.

Over the years I have had the good fortune of working with noted journalist and author Carlo Wolff. I learned more about writing in a five-minute conversation with him than I did in any classroom and follow his advice to this day. We strongly encourage you to read anything with his byline.

Also, special recognition to a guy who's known as "radio best friend", a title he's earned many times over. Art Vuolo has been documenting the history of radio for decades and preserved some of the most amazing talents in the medium on audio and video, a history that would have been lost without his foresight and effort. (We did a documentary about Cleveland FM radio a few years back titled *Radio Daze* that won a regional Emmy. We included some of Art's amazing video and…not intentionally…failed to include his great contribution in the credits!) The documentary would not have been nearly as successful without his fine work, and we sincerely thank Art for keeping radio history alive.

Our thanks also to Cliff Baechle, Tom Baechle, Brad Funk, Eric Funk, David Gray, Rick Funk, Martin Grams, Jr., Frank Kolar, Lorraine Kolar, Angelina Leas, Miriam Linna, Anthony Marotto, Bianca Marotto, Dennis Matz, Nancy Hribar Matz, Marilyn McKean,

Stuart Mintz, Cate Misciagna, Cole Misciagna, Cora Misciagna, Jenny Misciagna, Tony Misciagna, Carl Monday, Sandy Monday, Ben Ohmert and Bear Manor Media, Landen Phillips, Matt Phillips, Theresa Phillips, Michael Purhiser and Nick Talevski.

Introduction

We lived in a different world after WWII, and Cleveland, Ohio, was a good example. Gen Xers and Millennials might find that era confusing and even a little scary. Most people smoked, cars didn't have seat belts and mothers carried babies on their laps during the ride (maybe with a cigarette in their mouths). Often if you got stopped for drunk driving the police would just escort you home. You loved the smell of gasoline when you stopped to fill up, industrial smoke belched from factories and poultry hung in butcher shop windows. That smoke meant jobs, good paying work, and Roosevelt's dream of post war prosperity and "a chicken in every pot" could be seen on a simple stroll to the corner store. Boys had a wide array of toy guns to pick from and girls were pushed into traditional housewife roles. It was a world where kids ran around with white hot sparklers on the fourth of July, we had chemistry sets and woodburning kits and a whole range of potentially deadly things to pass the time. Think you live in a conservative world now? Post-war America was generally racist, anti-Semitic and sexist. Back in the fifties and sixties if you were a white protestant male you had it made. Other than that, you were on your own.

Big changes on the home front, too. There was that "TV thing", a big box with glowing tubes that gradually warmed up with an electronic hum that eventually showed a test pattern, usually a picture of an Indian, for the folks at home to tune in the clearest picture. The price of sets was costly at first but slowly coming down. There was more programming added by the week and a sure sign of affluence after the world war was an antenna on your roof. There was a big change among young people as well. Prior to the war it was likely you would grow up as miniature versions of your parents. You wore the same style clothes, shared the same home environment and listened to the same music on the radio. But after the war we saw more teenagers getting jobs, dressing differently, buying cars and hitting the road. It was the birth of a new youth culture, and Top 40 radio was the rising star that drew them all together.

The "Golden Age of Radio" came to a quick end when TV took off. Dad came home for dinner, maybe read the paper and turned on the television for the rest of the night. As a general rule mom and the rest of the family joined him…that is if the kids didn't have wheels. But much of the programming was simply a clone of popular radio shows, the comedies and dramas, with some even simulcasting. The entertainment your parents had didn't fit the younger lifestyle of driving down the road with your friends, the wind in your hair and flicking ciggies out the window.

Local radio felt the hit first and hardest. With ad money going to TV the industry needed something to bring people back and the older folks were watching fuzzy black and white screens. Radio staffs were cut, but programmers saw gold in a new type of entertainment. Rhythm and blues used to be called "race music". Remember what we said about racism back then? White kids were listening to songs by black artists, but in what some parents hoped to be a lily-white world that was a red flag. It wasn't long before programmers and record store owners like Leo Mintz at Cleveland's Record Rendezvous saw the potential and it was the sounding gun for what would eventually be called a "generation gap". Mintz would be a key link to the main players in this story as well as the history of rock and roll.

It was also fueled by the emerging post war youth culture. Remember those TVs we mentioned? Kids took to cars to get away from mom and dad who were glued to their sets. Why sit at home watching Jack Benny and Fred Allen when you could hit the open road and listen to Little Richard, Etta James and Ike Turner? It was a major concern for many parents. They saw it as a threat to the traditional American family they watched on "Father Knows Best" and "Ozzie and Harriet". (For those who can, think back. How many of your families even came close to that?) But there was another threat. Radio spawned a new kind of entertainer, the disc jockey spinning hits and speaking a language that kids understood, and parents found threatening. They pushed the youth movement with products and music and did it yelling into a microphone at a hundred miles an hour. In the Red Scare days of the 1950s some likened it to a dog whistle, something that only a select audience could hear and if it excluded adults it had to be evil. Welcome to a lifestyle that was based on rhythm and blues with a new name. Rock and roll.

Pretty soon white artists emulated black entertainers. In Memphis, Sun Records founder Sam Phillips was quoted as saying his formula for success centered on a simple phrase: "If I could find a white man who had the Negro sound and the Negro feel, I could make a billion dollars!" That was the way a lot of people spoke back then, especially in the Deep South, and Phillips found his model in Elvis Presley. The man who would be "King" shook the foundations of music as we had known it as well as his hips, and opened the door for Jerry Lee Lewis, Roy Orbison and so many others who charged to the top of the charts. You couldn't escape rock and roll, and when parents rose up against it the music became even more popular. Nothing tastes better than forbidden fruit. The folks bringing us that music? You guessed it. The disc jockeys.

Cleveland had some of the best. Carl Reese, "The Big Chief" Norm Wain, Alan Freed, Soupy Sales, Casey Qasem (and before you ask, yes. He did Anglicize his last name to Kasem) and for a time the most influential man in the early stages of rock and roll radio, Bill Randle. *Time* magazine called Randle the most important disc jockey in America back in the fifties, but fame comes and goes. Sadly, many of those names and the jocks that followed have been forgotten. Out of sight (or ear range), out of mind. That's the reason for this book. There was one Cleveland disc jockey who had a profound influence on local radio and even television who has faded into history. Pete Myers, who also performed under an alter ego. The Mad Daddy.

Let's make it clear that this book is primarily the story of Pete "Mad Daddy" Myers, but to have a greater understanding of his very complex character you also have to look at his influences, his contemporaries and the times they lived in. We tell his story through the words of the people who knew him as well as the publicity he generated. Work began on this project years ago, as a master's thesis believe it or not, and many of the people we spoke to were getting on in years and gave their final interviews. Their history and opinions about a troubled yet gifted performer live on in these pages. Was it a challenge? You'd better believe it was a challenge. Keep in mind that Myers was active from the fifties through the late sixties. There's no film of him as Mad Daddy and very little tape of his shows. Plus, he worked on air both as "lovable, laughable Pete Myers" and the Mad Daddy. Much of our research was based on print and the oral histories of the people who experienced his radio work.

We'll also look at the parallel paths shared by Myers and Alan Freed. Both got their first steps in big-time radio in Akron, landed at different times at Cleveland's WJW and WINS in New York, and played so-called "race records" …actually rhythm and blues artists… to a predominantly white audience during the often-polarizing struggle for civil rights and racial equality. Both were forced off the air for a time and were compelled to keep their names in front of the public until they could return with a vengeance. We also look at Freed, the announcer / promoter / pitch man vs. Myers, the announcer / entertainer. Both also shared tragic ends to their careers, yet Freed is regarded as one of the most important figures in the history of early rock and roll while Myers…well, let's just say he has yet to be discovered by a wider audience. Hopefully, this book will bring his story to greater prominence and understanding.

The other major influence on both these performers was the man often forgotten in the history of rock and roll radio and that's Leo Mintz. Mintz was a record store owner who knew what people wanted and, more importantly, what sold and how to do it. He had an ear for music, was a keen observer of teenage trends and very deep pockets. We'll also look at his important role in bridging racial divides through music and helping to redefine popular entertainment.

Let's take that big step back into time and meet our key players, but especially a benevolent Jekyll and Hyde who lived life at the speed of light and offered to take you along for the ride. Plenty took that offer, too.

Ladies and gentlemen…the Mad Daddy.

Janice & Mike Olszewski
Summer, 2023

Chapter One

"A Brazen Affront to our National Conscience"

The story really begins with the music itself, the starting gun that shook society around the world as youth realized its influence and potential. In the years following World War II, Cleveland was still a growing metropolis with over 900,000 people, the seventh biggest city in the U.S. It carried a wide range of ethnic and racial influences, each with their own neighborhoods, but still influencing all fueled in great part by the boom in electronic media. There was a time in Cleveland where immigrants could relocate to certain heavily ethnic areas and never need to learn English. Their native tongues were used by shop owners, tavern keepers, churches and even neighborhood newspapers. Many of these first-generation emigres learned just enough English to get by, usually on the job, and often with a healthy dose of profanity. Electronic media would serve not only as entertainment but as a teacher offering a look at other cultures and uniting the audience with a common language and vision.

Television was taking baby steps into American homes and while post-war prosperity was flexing its muscle on the home front it was a different story in Great Britain. We tend to forget that the war was pretty much fought in their backyard overseas and their road to rebuilding and recovery was far more complex and much slower. Their media was also far more restricted and strictly controlled while the American model was based to a great degree on free enterprise and commerce. Reception of Radio Luxembourg and the sea faring British pirate station Radio Caroline helped stretch those boundaries, but the U.K. was far behind most countries of the world in the way it offered its stations and programming. Despite that, the youth of America and Europe shared a common bond in the search for a more equitable, creative and tolerant general society. Music delivered that message.

Keep in mind that prior to the second World War American society was guided by tradition and strong family background. You grew up as miniature versions of your parents with the same values, clothing and even entertainment. Rebellion was not as common, though there were some who acted outside the norm usually based on lower economic status. (Maybe the Bowery Boys films serve as whimsical photos of that time. Famed comic artist Jack Kirby was another example, basing the wise cracking punks who tormented the *Fantastic Four*'s "Thing" on real life characters from his early life on Manhattan's Lower East side). But the post war boom years extended to the younger set as well as youth started to define its own culture with a move toward individuality, originality and independence with popular music as a springboard. It was the birth of "cool" and by the early 1950s Hollywood names like Marlon Brando, Natalie Wood, Sal Mineo and especially James Dean exploited that sense of image and rebellion. In a sense, if it was different and your parents didn't like it, chances were it was "cool" and that was a rallying cry.

The concept of "cool" was more than a badge of honor. It soon became a requirement. As historian and columnist Aurelio Icasiano III notes in his piece published in the online *Mantle* magazine, many in the older generation seemed to follow an ideal set by TV shows like *Father Knows Best* (1954) and *The Adventures of Ozzie and Harriet* (1952), both which had early incarnations in the waning days of radio's golden age. Financially secure families with high moral values safe in suburbia with no inner conflict became a mainstream ideal. But that wasn't real life for so many and Hollywood showed that other side. America was united during the war in a union that crossed racial, economic, religious and social lines. Nothing brings a group together like a common enemy. In an effort to unite the country post-war some power crazed politicians stressed the threat of Communism under every rock, though Hollywood's rebellious icons saw other options that shook the family unit, and that was the dysfunctional family that was a lot more common than shown in media. Perhaps misguided youth influenced by the influx of media and heading to widespread juvenile delinquency was the real threat to the American way of life. Even the F.B.I.'s J. Edgar Hoover jumped on the bandwagon led by Tennessee Senator Estates Kefauver to decry media "which flaunt decency and applaud lawlessness" in what was described as a "brazen affront to our national conscience".

Media could and did work both ways as Hollywood showed (and again, exploited) this behavior to an appreciative audience while other media stressed its effects on the so-called "adolescent subculture". Richard Gehman warned in the pages of *Cosmopolitan* about "a vast determined band of blue-jeaned storm troopers" and if that wasn't enough to bring back recent nightmares from overseas there were signs that young people with disposable income would lead to greater access of the most available, increasingly popular and often forbidden media. Records and music, and in a largely racist America, which was black based R & B.

Hollywood also picked up on that and saw profit in essentially "marketing rebellion", but to be perfectly honest so did the recording industry. Each had its own advantage. The visual aspects of film sold in a way that "a picture is worth a thousand words", but words were also a powerful tool in this marketing effort, especially as youth developed their own language patterns foreign to adults. A lot of that was based on musical slang with thinly veiled references to sex and "lifestyle". Samuel Z.Arkoff's low-budget American International Pictures was a popular source for much of that terminology well into the 1960s.

However, that wasn't just happening on the big screen. It was what came out of your car's radio speakers that had an even greater impact. The bebop jazz lingo of previous years had been seen as a novelty and in many ways even comic, but by the 1950s the new slang was more commonly used and to some even carried that sinister sub-meaning we mentioned.

Before we continue let's look at the origin of the term "rock 'n' roll". It's pretty well known that it was a euphemism for sex in some of the so-called race records, but it was in use even before that in a more general sense. Along with a distinguished career writing some of television's most honored comedies, Dan O'Shannon is also a noted pop historian and researcher. He found a reference in the radio listings in the November 13, 1934, edition of the *Cleveland Plain Dealer* stating, "Lou Rich's Ensemble headlines 'Rock and Roll' from Trans-Atlantic Merry Go Round in a show from WHK at 7:30 tonight". The WHK format at the time would hardly venture into anything close to R & B, but it's evident that the term signified some type of energetic performance, though fans of race records might have passed it on with a wink and a nudge. That same year, the Boswell Sisters released a tune titled "Rock and Roll" on the Brunswick label that was featured in the movie, *Transatlantic Merry-Go-Round*, referenced in the WHK show though their lyrics would seem to have more of a nautical theme.

The emerging popularity of race records simply brought many of those commonly used terms in black society to a greater audience and white America saw that as a distinct threat. The energy of black artists singing songs with veiled and sometimes blatant references to sex reaching out to a wide audience that included whites were seen as incredibly "cool" by young listeners, and potentially dangerous by the older generation. There was also a growing interest in folk music, often on college campuses, and some of the more diligent followers were discovering the music of Ma Rainey, Tampa Red and, of course, Robert Johnson among others that were rich with double entendre.

Cleveland's diverse population offered prime opportunities to find that brand of entertainment. When southern black families moved to Ohio in search of work and a better and more secure life, they brought their music and culture as well, adding to the ethnic influences that had already been established. Juke joints and house parties brought that tradition up north and Cleveland's inner-city neighborhoods reaped the benefits. With the right opportunities, music crossed the cultural barriers. Leo Mintz saw that early on.

Let's also take a moment to stress the importance of Mintz to the Cleveland radio scene and rock and roll in general. Fortunately, he has not been totally forgotten thanks in great part to the successful campaign to bring the Rock and Roll Hall of Fame to Cleveland. The story goes that Mintz took work as a pawnbroker after graduating from Cleveland's East Tech and he had an epiphany in 1938. After listening to the radio during a ride in the family car he announced to his wife, Betty, "I've got an idea! I'm going into the record business!" Let's just say Betty was a tad skeptical of the plan.

Mintz rented 214 Prospect Avenue in Cleveland as his first base of operations, a little store front and the owner of the building shared Betty's concerns. In fact, he told Mintz, "I won't lease the building to you because you won't last two months in the record business. I'll just rent you the property one month at a time." Mintz knew a good deal and with his entire life savings at the time, about $500, Record Rendezvous was born. Keep in mind that Cleveland's Prospect Avenue was a well-traveled street but didn't have the prestige or traffic seen just one block over on Euclid Avenue. You would need innovative ideas to lure in the shoppers, and as it turned out Mintz was the guy to do just that.

You should remember that records were usually sitting on a rack or shelf on a department store or "five and dime". You asked for something you heard on the radio, but Mintz put the records on display making it essentially a self-service store. He also made the rounds of taverns as far away as Columbus buying used jukebox 45s and 78s for pennies and selling them for a quarter. In fact, his initial business was dealing exclusively in used records. Then, another major innovation, the private listening booth. It happened in 1941, a first for the retail record industry, and a major draw for young buyers with money to burn. What also brought them in? The magic of radio.

By 1945, Mintz was buying radio time and that's critical to the story because it not only promoted the store and its mission but would also eventually underwrite both Alan Freed's and Pete Myers' Mad Daddy shows on WJW. More on that later on. It wasn't long before Mintz needed a much larger space and one opened up just a few doors away at 300 Prospect where he opened the new store in 1945. Let's keep in mind that rock and roll had yet to make its official debut, but so called "race records", those R & B sides with often suggestive lyrics, were paving the way to that end. Even so, he doubled his retail space with the move, but Mintz had what all the early architects of rock and roll marketing seemed to have and that was a keen ear for hits. Mintz knew what would sell and it wasn't long before word got out to producers and other record people that he was the "go to guy" to move product. Years later, Motown's Berry Gordy and producer Quincy Jones, who in his early career was hawking records, would pay tribute to Mintz at the Rock Hall's opening ceremonies. In fact, in the 1980s Jones could still fondly recall the exact route he would take from Cleveland's Union Terminal train station to Record Rendezvous on his way to the all-important meetings with Leo Mintz.

The store was also the place to be seen not only by its usually young customers but by artists themselves. In that era of late 40s and early 50s music the biggest stars playing Cleveland paid respects by "visiting the 'vous". Keep in mind that the stars included people like Rosemary Clooney, Milton Berle, Sarah Vaughn, Woody Herman and others, but that was the state of popular music at the time. It was also about to change with Mintz' help, and it started with a phone call.

Plenty has been written about another key player in this story, Alan Freed, and a good part has been passed on as legend thanks the Hollywood which also exploited the early youth rebellion. We'll come back to him through this history with a hard look at his "overnight success" that actually took several years, his influence on radio and rock and roll and his disastrous end in a face-off against hardline conservative America. In so many ways it reflects the tragedy of Pete Myers.

Let's take a quick a quick look at Alfred James "Alan" Freed. Born in Pennsylvania, his family relocated to Salem, Ohio, where his dad, Charles, ran a clothing business. Young Alan had a passion for flashy clothes and would be known for his white raincoats later on, but he always dressed sharply. It was pretty evident right from the start that Freed had a career in radio in mind. He claimed. "I drove my folks batty by reading the newspaper aloud for practice." Freed was good in sports as well as a talented trombone player. After he graduated from Salem High School in 1940, he spent two years at the Ohio State University until he landed his first radio gig for $17 a week at WKST-AM in New Castle, Pennsylvania, before moving on to WKBN-AM in Youngstown, and in June 1945 a major step to WAKR-AM in Akron.

Within months of his arrival, Freed was already getting some positive ink. January 1946 saw a feature story in the *Akron Beacon Journal* trumpeting the popularity of his late night "Request Review" record show aimed squarely at the so-called "bobbysoxers". Request shows had become really popular with kids sending in dedications often anonymously or with code names like "secret admirer", but one night Freed put a twist on the format by cracking the mic and singing along with Stan Kenton's "Tampico" At this critical point, the 23-year-old Freed started to develop as an outspoken radio personality focusing on young listeners with expendable cash the sponsors loved. Keep in mind this was a late show starting at 11:15 p.m. which made it even more attractive to kids who were supposed to be "sawing wood".

With the freedom to ad lib, the show offered Freed plenty of opportunities to plug his sponsors and offer his own unique code words and lingo. "Your Father's Mustache", "Danny Boy", "Little Dale" and "Londonderry Hair" made their way onto the streets showing you listened to "Request Review", with Freed getting more than 500 letters, telegrams, packages and postcards a day. This was in addition to his afternoon "Jukebox Serenade" show and his booth announcing work, so it was a full day on the job. Alan Freed fan clubs started popping up in high schools across the listening area. There were phone calls, too.

One of the odder requests came from a mother who couldn't get her baby to sleep. She asked Freed to sing a lullaby and he was happy to oblige…but the baby apparently wanted to hear the rest of the show.

There's an interesting twist to this story. Freed had some competition. It was his brother, Charles, who Alan saw as his earliest inspiration and was director of serious music at the Columbia radio network. On Wednesday nights between 11:30 and midnight the brothers went head-to-head with Charles directing the more highbrow "Invitation to Music" heard on crosstown WADC-AM. In truth, two different audiences but there may have been a curiosity factor to hear brother against brother.

WAKR was owned by the Berks, Bernard and Viola, and they took a liking to Freed. His first wife, Betty Lou, was ill and they had a couple of kids so Freed could use all the help he could get, and the Berks opened plenty of doors for him. That included "talent fees" from other shows, and Freed started to get visits from record label reps offering "gifts" to get their records played. It could be a bottle of booze, or maybe something the Berks didn't know about, but generosity often paid dividends. That's the way the record industry worked.

Freed wore a lot of hats at WAKR. By 1947 he'd called sports games, and even did classical music providing commentary for the Akron Symphony concert at the Goodyear Theater that May. But he also saw the winds of change on the popular music charts, and to be perfectly honest the record guys pushed product. Freed told the *Beacon Journal*'s radio editor, Bee Offineer, that "people are reaching for something new all the time. That accounts for the popularity of 'Heartaches' and 'Open the Door'." Freed also pointed to the Harmonicats "Peg O' My Heart" claiming he received 122 calls in just a half an hour after he played it for the first time, though five callers said they didn't care for the tune. Others were said to be "wholeheartedly enthusiastic." The Harmonicats, as the name suggests, were a harmonica group that today would be seen as a novelty act at best. But on that same page was an ad for "hit record releases" from Akron's Edfred's Record Shop on East Mill Street. It listed albums and 78s by category and artists ranging from barber shop melodies to hillbilly to blues – race music. They sold titles including "Across the Alley from the Alamo" by the Mills Brothers and Minnie Pearl's "I'm Lookin' for a Feller", but the titles of the "race records" told a different story with "Salty Papa Blues" by Dinah Washington and "Hamtramck Mama" by the York Brothers which had a decidedly country twang.

There were some stumbles. The Berks liked Freed, but they had a business to run, and they experimented a bit with the programming at the end of June 1947. Paul Whiteman was the "King of Jazz" back in the 20s and 30s. Balding, kind of pudgy, but he knew how to swing a baton and helped bring jazz to a greater audience. He was still a name, and the ABC radio network decided to give him a shot as a disc jockey. The first shows had guests like Ethel Merman and a singer that Benny Goodman discovered, Art Lund. Believe it or not, those names were still a draw and WAKR picked up the 3:30 show, dropping Freed's afternoon "Request Matinee". Fans of the early show were not happy. Neither was Freed.

Radio was continuing to change and so was its audience. Young people have always had a reputation for being "early adapters" and willing to try things that are new and innovative. Radio had been around for more than a quarter century, but the new role of the disc jockey presented a fresh use of the medium. Freed set his sights on the youth market early on, and in October 1947 he started broadcasting his "Radio Request" show from Akron's popular Jay-Teen club. Along with playing the hits he promised "stunts and contests" as an outlet for the youthful enthusiasm of the so-called "bobby soxers". Freed was among the first to have a studio audience, and as he put it, "If the boys and girls are in the studio, they aren't out in the streets getting into trouble " Meanwhile, on Mill Street, Edfred's Record Shop was advertising the latest race records aimed for a wide audience including, Clarence Samuels' "Lolly Pop Mama" and "Drummer Man Blues".

It wasn't long before Freed started promoting live stage shows, but they were a far cry from the concerts that would add to his infamy. For example, his January 1948 headliners were Jerry Murad's Harmonicats in two shows, matinee and evening, at the Akron Armory. The Harmonicats got plenty of airplay on Freed's radio gig and featured Lorain, Ohio, native Don Les who was born blind. And what a lineup of supporting acts! Akron's own Ross Halamay Orchestra, fellow Akronites the Woodson Sisters fresh from a USO dancing tour, and comedian Johnny Gallus from Earl Carroll's Vanities, plus on the early show a "local vocalist" contest with 200 singers from the region competing for fame and prizes. Five would win a spot on the evening show. It had all the trappings of an old-time vaudeville show. Oh, and that Whiteman thing? It didn't work out.

Kids wanted the hits and not Paul Whiteman waxing nostalgic about the good old days from before they were born. Maybe more importantly, the sponsors had enough and in June '48 Alan Freed's "Request Matinee" was back on the air. Akron wasn't unique. Whiteman's show went down hard from coast to coast and the network even tried different hosts. A look at the daily radio listings showed Freed had his hands full, but those hands brought in money. He did the "Request Matinee" for an hour, but also had a 25-minute show called "JukeBox Serenade" and then "Music for Dinner" for another 25-minutes. Add to that another three hours of "Request Matinee" on Saturday and two hours and 15-minutes for the weekend version of "Music for Dinner" and that adds up to another five plus hours. Keep in mind that Freed programmed his own shows. He chose all the records. It wasn't uncommon, but it was a practice that would come back to haunt him and some others in the years to come.

With all that exposure, Freed had established a firm hold on the greater Akron audience. While Arthur Godfrey dominated the second annual *Akron Beacon Journal* radio poll that March, Alan Freed's "Request Review" took top honors for Favorite Local Show beating the newspaper's own *Quizdown* program followed by *Dinner Winner*. Okay, weird titles but that was common in that era of radio. He was a big enough star that when Freed went on vacation it made headlines so fans wouldn't swamp the station with calls asking about the missing host of "Request Matinee" early in the day and the aforementioned "Request Review" that night. But it was soon evident that not everything Freed touched turned to gold.

His first marriage to Betty Lou went up in smoke in December '49, but he wouldn't stay single very long. Then, five years into his stay at WAKR, and maybe still feeling a bit miffed over the Paul Whiteman situation, Freed decided to spread his wings and in early 1950 accepted an offer from crosstown WADC-AM. It was a bad move, and one that would cost Freed dearly. Let's just say the Berks didn't care for that idea.

In February 1950, shortly after his first broadcast on WADC… which was just one hour… their attorneys swooped in and won a temporary injunction waving a "non-compete" clause in Freed's face. They called it a breach of contract and said the agreement he signed clearly barred Freed for an entire year from broadcasting from any station within 75 miles of Akron. Now, Freed's attorney took an interesting stand. His client had a family and needed the work and stressed that Freed did not work for WADC. He worked for an advertising firm, the Lew Platt Agency, and they brokered the time on WADC with Freed as their voice. That was a stretch and the judge sided with the Berks. Also, remember the name Lew Platt. He plays a critical role in Freed's rise to stardom. There was another hearing, on a Saturday, and the judge said even though Freed could be identified more accurately as a salesman rather than entertainer, he still couldn't broadcast within the 75-mile radius. Freed planned to appeal, but attorneys cost money and there was even some thought he would need to appeal to his audience for the funding to continue his fight. Freed defiantly announced, "I'll be back on the air in Akron, and you can bet your last nickel on that". The Berks were very successful and had a war chest to fund their legal team. Freed might soon be looking at his last nickel.

Until he could get the go ahead to go back on the air Freed needed work. Radio wasn't going to happen so the only option he had in the Akron – Cleveland market was TV which, frankly, at that time paid peanuts. TV sets were very expensive, few homes had them, but at that point it was any port in a storm. That March he landed a gig at Cleveland's Channel 9, WXEL-TV, doing three one hour shows after the Monday, Wednesday and Friday 11 p.m. news. Whether it was his idea or the station's, *The Alan Freed Variety Show* was scheduled for three hours per show until 2 a.m. He also had another iron in the fire.

Freed's next move may have been one of desperation. Let's face it, a guy has to make a living and his forced furlough provided a challenge to keep his name in front of the public. By March 1950, Freed had a well-established name in the Akron radio market and capitalized on that name by establishing the "Alan Freed School of Radio, Television and Public Speaking", a trade school introducing young hopefuls (who could afford the tuition) to an exciting career in broadcasting in just six weeks. It was located in the Metropolitan Building next to Akron's Palace Theater at 39 South Main Street. Freed took out large ads in the *Beacon Journal* promising intensive training in "radio announcing, public speaking, television sales presentation, poise, diction, radio and television writing, dramatics, production direction, professional singers (sic) microphone, and television camera technique." All "Under the Personal Guidance of Alan Freed". With all due respect to the apparent headmaster, he may have stretched himself pretty thin if there were enough applicants to keep the school afloat. Prospective students were encouraged to, "Prepare yourself now for a wonderful career in radio and television through the personal instruction of Alan Freed…

considered one of the Midwest's outstanding radio personalities and soon to star in his own television show." Let's pause and reflect for a moment. Freed had yet to host his own TV program, but he was offering to share his wide range of experience. It was a night class with limited seating, access to the latest radio and television facilities and the clincher, "exceptionally low pay as you learn rates." But it wasn't just for broadcast candidates. The evening classes also offered instruction in public speaking "especially designed for businessmen and businesswomen, club and lodge members, and all who make personal contact with the public." Applicants were told, "Remember! To learn the television profession the right way – Learn the Alan Freed way!" There was the David Freed way, too. His younger brother was wrapping up a radio production degree at Kent State University and agreed to help teach classes.

Just one month later the school had new studios and offices at the Portage Hotel at 10 North Main Street. The hotel was a favorite for local labor leaders who would meet at its popular Rubber Room Bar, and the opening of the new facility had Freed promising individual as well as class training in radio, television and public speaking. Once again, it offered intensive training in expanded facilities stating, "young men and women will find lucrative careers in radio and television." There was also an appeal for "singers – and men and women of all ages" encouraging them to "inquire about Alan Freed's personal and private instruction" stressing he could help attendees to "overcome self-consciousness and develop your personality". Offices were open from noon to 9 p.m., and sadly, the school wasn't around very long. There are no records of any of its students getting media jobs or even if any graduated. One of its phone numbers may have been an omen. It was Hemlock 1428.

Amid all of this turmoil, Freed took another wife just months after the end of his first marriage. Marjorie Hess showed a lot of faith in her husband entering a marriage to someone who was "between jobs". The Ninth District Appellate Court didn't do him any favors either. They upheld the ruling in favor of the Berks and

Freed hoped the Ohio Supreme Court would see his way. Until that happened, to supplement his income, Alan Freed took a part-time job as a bartender at the Kent Hotel near the university where his brother graduated. It took a year, but in March '51 the Ohio Supreme Court declined to review the case saying the contract stood. At that point it didn't matter because the non-compete had expired and Freed was back on WADC, and he hit the ground running.

There was a 4:30 record show daily, but it was what was happening at night that drew stares. WADC had him do a live record show from Ted Boyer's club, though a producer spun the discs back at WADC between Freed's live remote breaks. Oh, and he was keeping the TV show, too. The next month a full-page ad in the *Akron Beacon Journal* showed a beaming Alan Freed promising "interviews and music broadcast nightly midnight to 1 o'clock over WADC" from the Candle-Lite Drive Inn restaurant, home of Peanutburgers, jumbo shrimp and bottomless cups of coffee. It featured crystal pendant chandeliers, Russell Wright dinnerware and, of course, "Alan Freed's Forum" interviewing late night patrons live on the air…starting at midnight. You read that right. After a year of struggle, Freed wasn't about to quibble over paying hours.

Despite his return to the Akron airwaves on WADC and his continuing presence on Cleveland TV at WXEL, Freed was forced to file for bankruptcy in May 1951. Freed claimed more than $4700 in debt with just $100 to his name. His 1950 Dodge was worth about $1300, but he had two liens for $1800. Plus, he owed his attorney John Russell $2100 for legal fees and a personal loan. He listed two places of employment, WADC and Cleveland's WXEL-TV. Still, there was some possible light on the horizon. He had heard about this guy up north who might help him out.

Even before he took the WADC job, Freed had phoned Leo Mintz about helping him find work in Cleveland radio. Mintz listened to an aircheck, heard potential and was able to get Freed in at WJW. Record Rendezvous had advertising muscle and a call from Mintz went right to the top. Betty Mintz recalled, "Alan was a cocky kid, a real go-getter." Mintz liked ambition and with the right direction everyone would profit. By July 11th, after just a few weeks on WADC, Freed debuted on Cleveland's "Chief" station. A tape of a 1973 interview with Leo Mintz aired on WMMS, and he described those first meetings with Freed.

Mintz recalled, "He worked at a radio station in Akron, Ohio… as a disc jockey. He was terrific! They were paying him about $45-50-60-100 dollars a week and he was very, very unhappy and he quit. But in his original contract he could not appear on any radio station within the radius of 35 miles. He came in to see me one night at my home…broke, dirty, miserable, hungry. Wanted to go to work for me somewhere, somehow. That was the year that Channel 8 (WXEL-TV) first started. We put him on TV for one year at a very small salary to wait out his expiration of the restrictive (contract). He played records on the TV, believe it or not." He also knew better things were ahead for Freed and himself with the proper venue and that was radio where Freed felt most comfortable. But Mintz also admitted Freed needed to focus on a new audience, saying, "When this period was over we put him on WHK (Author's note: It was actually WJW) … I forget the name of the manager of the station there…and Alan started to play Bing Crosby, Vaughn Monroe and all that sort of crap. I said, 'Who needs you to play this!?' We sell in our store downtown, we were the biggest store in the state at the time, records that were at that time called blues and rhythm. And I kept hollering, 'Alan, let's go this, let's do that. Let's play this., let's play that', and he still insisted on playing the Bing Crosby and Vaughn Monroe things. We sat down here one day in my office downstairs…we both got loaded. I said, 'Son of a bitch! If you can't make those people rock and roll we're dead!' And that's how that word was born!"

In an earlier interview with syndicated columnist Earl Wilson, Freed had a slightly different take. He told Wilson, "In June of 51, the Record Rendezvous sponsored me in Cleveland. Joe (sic) Mintz, the owner, a real sharpie, and I were kicking around names for shows. I'd started with rhythm-and-blues in Akron and was still living in Akron and commuting." Wilson pressed Freed asking, "You personally thought up the term?". Freed replied, "Whether he said it or I said it, I don't know. He predicted it would be the biggest thing in popular music, and it is. Anyway, we started the *Rock and Roll Dance Party* on WJW Radio." When asked earlier if the term had a double meaning, Freed pointed out, "Cole Porter's written double-meaning songs if you want to go into that. But why is it that every new popular music is accused of being immoral?"

Freed's move to 850 on the AM dial is well documented in books like John Jackson's well researched <u>Big Beat Heat</u> (Schirmer, 1995), but the eyewitness accounts from newspapers and trade publications of the day provide additional perspective. The original name for Freed's WJW show was *The Freeditorium*, but changed its name to *Moon-Dog House* when Mintz agreed to help underwrite it. In fact, there are reports that Mintz actually sat side by side with Freed at times in the WJW studios handing him platters to spin. The formula worked. Competing stations took notice as well, with WSRS (now WJMO) bringing in "The Hound Fog" George Lorenz from Buffalo, but they didn't have the ear, foresight, deep pockets or access to the music that Leo Mintz brought to the table.

These were the days of radio fan clubs and Alan Freed had fans in the thousands. They followed him to appearances at Moondog Balls in Akron, Canton and smaller towns with some reports of as many as 4000+ attending. A good part of Freed's success in radio and especially WJW came from his interaction with the public, fueled by his own growing ego. As it's been established over the years, the folks who brought you the music over the airwaves were as much a star as the acts they played and Freed basked in the spotlight. It wasn't long before Freed took hungry celebrities looking to get exposure to his shows on the road playing glorified sock hops but packing in the fans (and potential record buyers). Freed exploited his personae as "the Moondog" and his growing cadre of fans as his "Moondoggers". He'd staged the series of small hall Moondog balls and dances that drew packed house, but Freed took it upon himself to stage a show where he would be crowned the king of the Moondoggers and the date was set for March 21, 1952. The Moondog Coronation Ball would be held at the Cleveland Arena, and when tickets sold out practically overnight the promoters added a second show. Confident the show was in good hands, Mintz and his family boarded a plane to Florida for a vacation celebrating his son Stu's birthday. When the printer asked what the tickets should look like they were told, "just like the first set". What the promoter failed to say was the addition of the words "second show" and the time. In so many ways it was a near fatal mistake, and one that added greatly to the appeal of the music and Freed himself, when everyone showed up at the same time. Another person who ended up at the Arena that night? Leo Mintz, and he didn't like what he saw.

The writing was on the wall as early as the morning of the Arena show, if not before. When the mistake was finally noticed with no possible way to correct it that late in the process a panicked call was made to Mintz at his Florida home and he raced to the airport. Keep in mind that these were the days before commercial jets and Mintz hopscotched across the country on a day full of anxious layovers and racing to the next flight. He jumped in a cab when he arrived in Cleveland and the cabbie took him directly to the Arena where he surveyed the chaos firsthand. There were reports that Mintz never left the car but angrily spoke to Lew Platt and Milt Kulkin who saw him roll up. That may be urban legend, but there is one thing for certain: Mintz told the cabbie to head back to the airport and made a stop at the bar before boarding the plane back to Florida.

The *Plain Dealer* called it a "confined mass of humanity" with crowds knocking down doors and pushing the police side. People were jammed shoulder to shoulder with movement impossible. The paper claimed only one arrest, a 20-year-old from the city's west side, who was taken in for fighting supposedly when someone pulled his hair. Another concert goer, 25-year-old Emmet Greshan had a gouge taken out of his left cheek by a man yelling, "I'm coming through!". Fortunately, the wound was easily treated at nearby St. Vincent Charity Hospital. Shortly after the concert ended the crowds slowly dispersed, but not before giving that genre of music instant notoriety.

Freed later defended his role to Earl Wilson, claiming, "No, I don't consider them riots. Teenagers showing they liked music. The Cleveland Arena held 12,000 (Author's Note: Freed's numbers may be off.), we drew 30,000. I warned the Cleveland police that they ought to have every available man out on Euclid Avenue. They didn't pay attention, same as the New York police didn't at first. (Note: This regards the disturbance at Freed's Paramount Theater shows.) So, the doors gave in at the Cleveland Arena – and everybody got in for free." It would be more accurate to say anyone who didn't buy a ticket…legitimate or bootleg…got in that way.

Suddenly, Alan Freed and rock and roll had a reputation, a bad one, making it so much more attractive to a young rebellious audience.

Freed's old hometown newspaper, the *Salem News* ran headlines proclaiming, "Cleveland Dance Fails from Too Much Success", though it added that part of that event included two stabbings. Weeks later, *Broadcasting* magazine ran full page ads with a beaming Freed claiming, "Radio Alone Pulled 25,000!" thanks to WJW's *Moondog House* show. The ad also showed Freed standing with two black artists, snippets from local papers describing the melee, and strongly plugging WJW as Cleveland's best radio ad buy. Lemonade from lemons! It was such a publicity windfall that less than two months later a permit was issued by the city's safety department (despite the protests of Police Chief Frank W. Story) to stage yet another Moondog Ball at the Cleveland Arena that May, but not without certain guarantees. The city's law department found it had no legal basis to deny the permit, and it came with a promise from the Arena's manager J. C. Handy that only 6000 tickets would be issued for each of the three scheduled shows…. plainly marked with the appropriate times….and an additional 50 police would be on hand to maintain order. The announcement came on the heels of a $50,000 lawsuit filed against Freed and the promoters by the chart-topping quintet the Orioles who claimed Freed falsely advertised they would appear at the show in March. That wasn't the end of Freed's legal challenges, but that was the price of doing business.

Ads for Freed's "Moondog Maytime Ball" on May 17th and 18th promised "the greatest array of stars to ever appear on a combined show and dance" and at first glance it sure lived up to its name. The Dominoes topped the bill that included "H-Bomb" Ferguson, Al "Fats" Thomas, Joan Shaw, the Calvin Brothers, plus Todd Rhodes, Freddie Mitchell and Morris Lane with their respective orchestras. It should also be pointed out that Freed used Rhodes' King Records release "Blues for the Red Boy" for a time as his show's theme song. On that same lineup was a Cleveland native, "Little Jimmy" Scott, a former vocalist with the Lionel Hampton band who had a sort of androgynous quality about him due to a hereditary hormonal condition called Kallman syndrome. He never went through puberty and had a high, reedy, yet powerfully emotional voice that influenced everyone from Billie Holliday to Madonna and, after a serious lull in his career that had him doing everything from bussing tables to operating elevators at Cleveland's May Company, was rediscovered in the 1980s and even toured with Lou Reed and still later singing on David Lynch's *Twin Peaks* TV series in the 1990s.. All the proceedings, of course, were presented by the King of the Moondoggers himself.

More shows followed in rapid succession and in bigger venues. In the weeks to come Freed hosted shows with his "Caravan of Stars" at Cleveland's Public Auditorium with Woody Herman, the Mills Brothers and Dinah Washington along with Tommy Edwards and Herkie Styles. He filled the Akron Armory at his "Moondog Royal Ball" with Count Basie, the Moonglow and an 18-act roster with Freed's named listed bigger than any of the acts in the lineup. Point of interest: Along with the venue box offices these were the days when you could buy tickets at furniture and clothing stores, as well as record shops, which usually ran commercials on Freed's program. Not a bad trade off and extra bang for the advertising dollar.

It should also be pointed out that Freed was still a fixture on WXEL-TV and in September 1952, he found himself along with fellow staffer Grant Wilson filling in as hosts of a short film program. For that show, they both dressed as "cowpokes" which *Plain Dealer* columnist George Condon jokingly said showed just how versatile the two actually were.

Oddly enough, Freed's legacy came close to being cut short when he escaped a near fatal car crash. It happened on April 19, 1953, when Freed was returning home after a long day at WXEL followed by his usual high energy radio show. He fell asleep at the wheel and his car crashed into a tree in Shaker Heights leaving him with a broken arm, a ruptured spleen, and a severely lacerated face that took seven and a half hours of plastic surgery to repair. He spent the next three weeks at St. Luke's hospital, though he was originally expected to be there almost two months. Freed joked that, "I think I gave them so much trouble in the hospital that they were glad to get rid of me!", adding, "It gets awfully dull lying around all day with nothing to do." He also paused to reflect. While the doctors had yet to give him the go ahead to return to work, which would come soon enough, Freed admitted, "All I know is that I am a very, very lucky guy to here at all."

It's just about every broadcasters' dream to make it in New York and Freed was no exception. By July 1954, Freed had decided to relocate to WINS / New York where his star would soar in the nation's media capital. The decision made headlines in Cleveland, where *Plain Dealer* media writer George Condon quoted the industry bible, *Billboard*, as saying Freed's salary "may involve the biggest sum of money ever paid to a rhythm and blues jockey by an independent radio station". His last Cleveland show would be August 15. WJW's general manager William Lemmon vowed the *Moondog Show* would continue after Freed's departure, but he didn't mention if he might be buying the program from New York. The deal included a syndicated show, and many assumed it would air in his old hometown as well as overseas, though Lemmon sent a shot over the bough claiming WJW owned the "Moondog" label? and Freed would need the station's permission. It was unlikely that Freed would drop the name and there was a very good possibility that if WJW didn't air it in syndication another Cleveland station was waiting in the wings.

The loss of Freed obviously meant loss of revenue for WJW and the station wasn't about to make his transition an easy one. Attorneys on both sides of the naming issue started rattling their sabers. It was initially reported that Freed's show would be on WJW as part of an eight-city network, but according to GM Lemmon that included a verbal agreement the title *Moon Dog House* would be legally established property of the station by virtue of trademark. He claimed that included a deal that would give WJW a percentage of all profits generated by the show from all stations on the network outside of New York. That also meant any variation or breakdown of the title, including "King of the Moon Doggers", etc., would be considered a violation of the trademark and here come the lawsuits. But as they say, the devil can often be found in the fine print.

WINS' general manager Robert Lederer responded saying, "Upon investigation by our legal advisers in Washington, we found that WJW had registered the title, but did not have a trademark."

Ooooops!

"Our attorneys do not consider that the registration entitled WJW to a percentage arrangement since it does not actually constitute ownership." Lederer added, "We can't be expected to pay them for something they don't own." It was determined that the program would be *The Alan Freed Show*, but the host would continue to call himself, "The Moon Dog King". WINS essentially said, "Want to fight it out in court? We're right here!" Lederer also promised that Freed would be heard in Cleveland again, on WJW or another station, within weeks of his arrival in New York, but Lemmon had his own plans.

Freed's show was already known in the greater New York area having been rebroadcast on Newark's WNJR, and when a May 1st concert at the Sussex Armory there was announced it drew 18,000 ticket holders with another 6000 ready to push their way in. The lineup that night included Roost Bonnemera and his Mambo Band, vocalist Ella Johnson with Buddy Johnson and his Orchestra, the Clovers, jazz sax player Sam Butera, Nolan Lewis, the Harptones, Charles Brown and blues great Muddy Waters. A lot of talent for the ticket price. There was talk it would be recorded for a special Moondog album, and surprisingly a group of Clevelanders were supposed to travel there on a special train but, unfortunately, it had to be cancelled. There were too many requests! Fortunately, it was not a replay of the Moondog Coronation Ball at the Cleveland Arena. *Billboard* magazine named Freed the top R & B disc jockey in the country. The New York deal also included 52 episodes of a TV show to feature blues artists. Now all Freed had to do was get ratings. Big time.

Now, it's important to note that two key points in Freed's influence would result from this move, one sooner than the other. When Freed cracked the mic at WINS-AM that September (at a jaw dropping salary of $75,000 a year in 1954 dollars) he brought his love for the 1949 single "Moondog's Symphony" which he'd used as his theme song. Little problem here. The blind street artist who did that single for SMC Pro-Arte Records was alive and well and performing in New York. His birth name was Louis Hardin, and he filed a copyright infringement suit against Freed with some heavy hitters for the time…Benny Goodman and Arturo Toscanini… backing him up in court as to his musical influence. Hardin won and the radio show was rechristened as *Alan Freed's Rock and Roll Party*. In truth, back in his Cleveland days Freed had already been advised to stress the tunes as rock and roll rather than "moondog music" by Chuck Berry himself who had closely aligned himself with that title. Prior to that, Freed's old partner Leo Mintz was also said to have been the person who told Freed that white kids were "rockin' and rollin'" to so-called race records in the aisles of his store and is recognized as the first person to use that term for that genre of music before Freed.

Freed made the necessary change but tried to take it a step further. Along with Lew Platt (remember him?), WINS and a young night club operator named Morris Levy, Freed attempted to copyright the term "rock and roll", but by that time it was part of the entertainment lexicon so that attempt failed. Notice a key name that was not included in that request. Leo Mintz. Was there bad blood between them after Freed went to New York? Difficult to say because Freed was making a lot of money in Manhattan, but word got around that he was also asking certain folks for loans. Levy would go on to form Roulette Records and later be linked to one of New York's organized crime families.

Would Freed be successful in New York? Some had their doubts and, to be perfectly honest, most were his detractors. A January 1955 issue of *Variety* put the naysayers in their place. It reported that Freed personified the "big beat in the pop music biz", and his "Rock and Roll Party" at the St. Nicholas Arena was a prime example. The turnout was way over capacity and cops had their hands full holding back the crowds when the sell out crowd of 7500 made their way into the venue. Does that sound oddly familiar?

An interesting note: In the early days of rock and roll, Alan Freed would play an unwitting role in the development of the of a group of musicians who would be the vanguard of the so-called British Invasion that would repackage the black based music Freed championed. His show was syndicated to military bases across Europe and could be picked up by shortwave across most of England. It was music the British Broadcasting Corporation didn't offer, but young listeners knew where to find it and Freed had an international following. A top British TV "presenter" at the time was Carroll Levis, who hosted a talent show called *Search for a Star*. In 1958, still stinging from a failed audition for the program in Liverpool months before, a group called the Quarrymen traveled to Manchester for another try. However, at this point the group was down to three with the recent departure of Duff Lowe and Len Garry. They were for the time being a guitar trio, and for this audition…perhaps to shrug off the previous snub…decided to bill themselves as "Johnny and the Moondogs". Author Bob Spitz suggests they may have taken the name from broadcasts of Freed's *Moondog Show* out of Luxembourg. Improvising after the loss of two members, the group took the stage with a guitar on each end and the lead singer with his arms around the two. It worked! The audience reaction was registered by a "clapometer", and the trio was asked to the finals… but there was a problem. They couldn't stick around for the final competition because they had to catch the last train back to Liverpool. Not to worry. "Johnny" Lennon, George Harrison and Paul McCartney would pick up a drummer, refine their act even further and you know the rest.

While Freed's syndicated show initially got the green light to air on WJW, the station still had a stable of air talent, but who would (or frankly, could) replace the one-time "king of the Moondoggers"? Pete Myers was still years away from Cleveland, though his arrival at that time would have caused a sensation had he been ready. Instead, WJW gave one of its salespeople, Virgil Brinnon, a shot. He'd done some disc jockey work and did a three hour show nightly on WJW, with general manager Lemmon boasting fan mail for the show "increased significantly" since Freed's departure. Uh, yeah. Virg Brinnon was probably a very likable guy on and off the air…. but let's put the cards on the table… he's pretty much forgotten today. Even so, other stations saw an opening for that type of programming. *Plain Dealer* writer George Condon asked, "What did Cleveland radio listeners ever do to bring on this avalanche of 'rhythm and blues' programs in the late evening hours? Allan (sic) Freed's 'Moondog' program on WJW was the only show of its type here for several years, but now that Freed has departed for New

York, three stations are featuring the same type of show – WJW, WSRS, and WHK. The howling and caterwauling is something fierce."

By March of 1956, Freed was seen as one of the darlings of the still emerging sound in the biggest media market in the world with the CBS Radio Network announcing he would host a syndicated rock and roll show, but once again that adds to the drama as the Cleveland network affiliate was on WGAR. Time… and lawyers…. would determine who would carry the show if it ever made it to the air. It's important to bear in mind that Alan Freed's climb to the top weighed heavily on his own self-promotion. Sure, the music was different and maybe even perceived as dangerous and youth were emerging as a major social and cultural force, but Freed was able to…for lack of a better term…"exploit" the movement and rise to its leadership. He still had his detractors, and they often had a very loud voice. When the film, *Rock, Rock, Rock!* (1956) was released in December you would think the Northeast Ohio headlines would read, "Local Boy Makes Good". Not this time. The *Beacon Journal* review offered a tepid "Teenagers May Like It" and columnist Art Cullison proceeded to dissect it scene by scene. Admitting that he wasn't exactly a fan of the music, Cullison said it wasn't the rock and roll that made him hate the movie but because it was "just a cheap quickie thrown together in a hurry aimed at some fast cash" film. He called the storyline "idiotic" meant only to link the dozen rock acts and make it attractive to young music fans. Cullison also took aim at the production values calling the recording "unusually bad" and out of sync with the singers mouthing the lyrics. Fair enough and Vanguard Productions wasn't known for timeless classics like *Citizen Kane* (1941). He did like some of the acts praising Frankie Lymon, LaVern Baker and the Moonglows, and noted that Connie Francis actually sang the parts mouthed by the female co-star, Tuesday Weld, (with a cameo by future TV star Valerie Harper in a non-speaking role).

Cullison recognized Freed's early days in Akron saying he was the one "accused" of starting rock and roll steamroller. He also noted Freed had little to do with the film other than some dialogue and supposedly conducting the house band. As for the non-musical stars, Tony Randazzo and Miss Weld, the reviewer was hopeful, "They may become actors someday." By the way, the film did a huge box office! Take that, Art! There was another performer watching Freed's success from afar, and the time was fast approaching for him to make his move.

So, what do we know about this so-called "Mad Daddy"? Well, apparently, he was a born performer, and it may have run in the family. Myers' younger brother, Ernie, gained fame as a disc jockey in San Diego, though some say he also had his sights set on a career in movies. In fact, he played the role of the president in the film *Attack of the Killer Tomatoes* (1978) along with former WERE disc jockey and noted character actor Jack Riley. You'll remember Riley as the neurotic Elliot Carlin on *The Bob Newhart Show* (1972), though a younger generation would recognize him as the voice of Stu Pickles in the animated series, *Rugrats* (1991). Ernie Myers worked as an actor in New York in radio soap operas before a four-year stint in the army during the Korean War. His debut on San Diego radio was in 1954, but let's not get ahead of ourselves. What about the mysterious Pete Myers?

Pierre 'Pete' Myers was born in San Francisco in 1928, and according to Ernie had no hesitation in calling attention to himself. Ernie Myers claimed Pete had an I.Q. of 175. To put that in perspective, the average IQ is about 100 and Stephen Hawking was at 160 with Albert Einstein right around there. There's no official record of 175, but Pete was plenty bright, and wasn't afraid to take chances. Ernie told us in a phone interview that, "Pete was highly creative as a child, as well as a mischief maker. He wrote his own plays, one in which he played a WWII German submarine captain. He went to John Marshall High School, and two years later the Mark Ken School for professional kids." At the time, the prestigious Mark

Ken School was located on Franklin Boulevard in Los Angeles. A look at those who are exceptionally bright will also show they often look at conformity and rules as unnecessary boundaries, and Pete Myers is a prime example. Ernie also stressed that early on his brother, Pete, had a rebellious streak as well recalling, "He once stole a street sweeper, rode it down Hollywood Boulevard near Vine in Los Angeles and was picked up by the police. The principal told the cops, 'I guess you didn't have any problems spotting him!' The police let him go."

Pete Myers would eventually make his way to London, England, to pursue his dream for his own acting career. He studied at the Royal Academy of Dramatic Arts and was able to find occasional work as an actor before joining the Army. Pete Myers would later tell the *Cleveland Press* that, "I decided to attend the academy because I figured that when I went looking for a job it might impress the producers. It didn't even faze them. One thing I did while in London though was a command performance before Princess Margaret. I appeared as Orlando in "As You Like It". Impressive, but only one line on a resume.

Ernie Myers also mentioned that Pete loved eastern culture. The armed forces called and when he was stationed at Camp Drake in Japan during his time in the army in the late 1940s Pete often sent home kabuki souvenirs. That interest in eastern culture and philosophy was backed up by his future colleague Neil McIntyre who said, "He collected artwork and artifacts. He used to have it around his apartment. He was very interested in Japanese culture." Rites, tradition, honor, the role of the warrior. All held a fascination for Myers and may have had a profound effect on his psyche twenty years on. Japan is also where, as a corporal, he did some work for Armed Forces radio WVTR and television and caught the attention of an American icon. Let's just say the results were far from positive.

Myers and a supporting cast did a phony story… about a sea monster coming out of a bay near Tokyo! Unfortunately, General

Douglas MacArthur was visiting his son at a hospital, and heard the broadcast. He was not amused. MacArthur did not hear the warning that it was only a radio skit, which had Myers claiming troops were being mobilized to save Tokyo from a sea monster. You can imagine MacArthur blowing steam out of that corn cob pipe like Popeye. This was not the kind of programming you heard on the Armed Forces network. Failing to see the humor in that broadcast, Myers was transferred out of Tokyo on the general's orders and was put in a unit studying psychological warfare. Yeah, the irony in transferring to the psychological unit seems obvious.

While in Japan Myers also took a wife, the first of three times he would take a walk down the aisle. On December 27, 1950, Myers married Sylvia Burton Crane at St. Luke's Chapel at the American Hospital in Tokyo in a ceremony officiated by the Reverend Howard Hanaford. It was the same hospital where the bride was born when her father worked for the *Tokyo Moren*, the English-language newspaper, twenty years before and it was no surprise the wedding made the pages of the *New York Times* stateside since Burton Crane was now a correspondent for that paper. Following a reception at the Tokyo Correspondent's Club the couple sped off for a wedding trip to Kuwana just a few miles away. It should be pointed out that after graduating Wellesley College in 1947 the new Mrs. Myers was herself a well-known magazine correspondent for the *Saturday Evening Post,* while Myers was still listed as a civilian attached for General MacArthur in the psychological warfare section. The marriage would end a few years later in divorce. Even more changes were on the way.

The military life obviously didn't suit Myers and following his discharge he decided to aggressively pursue an acting career. Like a lot of struggling actors paying their dues, Myers took any job he could while going to endless auditions. McIntyre recalled, "When he came to New York City the first time, before he traveled back to California, he demonstrated toys at Macy's department store." There was something about the Big Apple that really appealed to him.

Still, Myers' first stay in New York might have been described as frustrating at best. He had limited success in a few stage productions and bit parts on Broadway, later finding work doing summer stock theater in the Catskills and as far away as St. Louis. Even so, he was also getting little attention from booking agents and producers, but he soldiered on with hopes that the next audition could open doors to a lasting career. The only thing that seemed to last was his unemployment, but why?

His talent seemed obvious. Myers was described as "a natural character actor with easy ethnic mimicry, broad face and fair hair." For a while he landed more bit parts in dramatic TV series such as *Project 90* (1953) and *You Are There* (1947), sometimes as a heel-clicking Nazi soldier. Years later he recalled, "I was popular with the *You are There* and *Eyewitnesses* series because it seemed that when it came to making like a German general I excelled. Of course, you can't make a living any longer playing a German because Nazis are no longer in vogue. Now it's the Russians."

But the acting gigs came few and far between, and Myers would find himself unemployed time and again. Frustrated by his lack of success, and not looking forward to another winter at Macy's toy department, he packed his bags in late 1956 and headed to see his brother Ernie who was now doing well as a disc jockey in San Diego.

Ernie Myers convinced Pete that media could be a perfect career fit, but there were a few stumbles. He recalled that Pete, "Co-anchored the TV news on KFSD Channel 10 in San Diego for a while in his early twenties. He got fired from that job." Ernie wasn't exactly sure of the circumstances that led to his dismissal, but if he was willing to do radio reports in Korea about giant lizards it would seem hard news wasn't his forte. But there was another guy with lofty radio aspirations who had a bit of a head start.

Chapter Two

Moondoggers

Myers finally decided to follow Ernie's lead by trying commercial radio. He landed a job for a time at KCBQ 1170 AM in San Diego, but it didn't fit his musical style or personality. He saw it as a job with little challenge, no future and worst of all, boring. Pete Myers hated to be bored. As he put it, "Disc jockeys and music aren't as popular in that area as they are in the east so I looked for a good market and picked Cleveland." The radio market back east, especially in Cleveland, was thriving and a great steppingstone. In 1957, Myers made a few calls, and soon after packed his belongings into his 1950 Packard and headed to WHKK / Akron. His arrival in the "Rubber City" came at a time when Akron was a much bigger radio market and offered additional opportunities for someone looking to fast track his media career.

It wasn't Cleveland, but Myers told his brother Ernie it was "Close enough for me!" He was also interested in trying the waters of television in a bigger market than San Diego and looked to comedian Ernie Kovacs as a prime example. Kovacs had gone from radio to television in Philadelphia, which at the time was a market similar in size to Cleveland. Recalling those days, Ernie Myers said Akron would play a profound role in his brother's development as a radio performer, saying, "He came up with the Mad Daddy character in Akron. Pete chose Akron because it was the first station to make him an offer, and it was a major step toward the much bigger market of Cleveland."

Upon his arrival in the Rubber City Myers did what a lot of single guys did, and he checked into a boarding house. Notice the word "single". There's no word how it happened but after a brief period Myers first marriage was now history. There was a "Room to Let" sign at 69 Beck Avenue in Akron's Highland Square district, and Myers moved into a third-floor walk-up. Mike Altimore and Travis Roudebush were two of his downstairs neighbors. Altimore remembers him well, saying, "He was on the radio at the time, and he was crazy! He didn't talk to us much because he was always on at night. But two other guys that worked at WAKR rented there, too. They were on the second floor with us, and we used to play cards a lot. They would go on in the morning. We worked during the day, too, because we had the barber shop. He always wore a black cape and he'd come in and swing it around before he went up the stairs. He never really talked to us much. When he came in, he went right up the steps. He was a loner pretty much. Not on the radio, but certainly by himself." Roudebush remembers the carefree days of young guys…but agrees that Myers separated himself from everyone else. "We used to have card games until 3 in the morning!", according to Roudebush. "Pete would come walking in, middle of the night. but he was in and out. He never played cards with us. He wouldn't even say hello. He would just go right up to his apartment. You had to go through the house to get to the third floor and he was staying in the maid's quarters. Yeah, he was a real character." And how do you define a character? "He would come home at night in that cape. Mike saw him in that get up more than I did. He was kind of scary. You didn't see guys walking around Akron in the middle of the night in capes! There were too many devils running around. We were all hiding! We used to listen to Pete when he was the Mad Daddy. He was a different guy on the radio, pretty crazy! He was as big a name as the records he played. Bigger!" But that didn't mean Myers didn't enjoy his time off the job. "One thing about Pete. I know he liked the grape. He drank a lot of wine at home. His trash barrel was always full of bottles."

Roudebush recalls, "Another deejay, Joe Finan, was his real friend. He got married at Joe's house up in Bay Village along the lake. Joe lived down the street from Dr. Sam Shepard, who got committed for killing his wife." "Shepard was the Bay Village doctor convicted in the bludgeoning death of his wife, Marilyn, spent a few years in prison and years later was later found not guilty in a defense led by famed attorney F. Lee Bailey. When he died of liver failure in April 1970 Shepard was pursuing a career as a professional wrestler. Back to Roudebush. "Pete met this blonde, he didn't know her very long, and they got married." While the circumstances regarding the end of his marriage to Sylvia Crane are uncertain, Myers took the time on March 29th to tie the knot with the second of his three wives, Ann Boyce. "He lived with us until then and then he was gone. Pete moved out to another place on Highland Square a little closer to downtown Akron."

Myers got a good deal of attention right off the bat at WHKK, if only for the nature of the music he was playing. Just weeks after his WHKK debut, Myers and other popular names across the Akron dial including WAKR's Scott Muni (later a pioneer in New York rock radio) and WCUE's Art Roberts (who was in Buffalo and Chicago) were displayed in photos above an article in the *Beacon Journal* with the provocative title, "Is It Music or Garbage? Even Those Pushing It Disgusted with 'Junk'". It was a combined effort of the *Beacon Journal* and the *Chicago Daily News* wire service and from the opening sentences focused on the corrupt manner that records companies pursued to get singles of questionable value airplay and, more importantly, into the hands of consumers. Its bias was evident right down to the photo of Elvis that was tagged, "Elvis Presley may sing garbage – but it sells". Historians today would argue that Presley's groundbreaking work with Sun Records was among his best and his output with RCA Victor laid the foundation for much of popular culture for decades to come.

The article starts out with a fictional chain-smoking executive at a small record label frantically doing whatever he can to get his product mentioned in the leading trade magazine *Cash Box*. It talked about "deals" with deejays from big markets to Covington, Kentucky, to add the records from his label. The record exec identified as 31-year-old "Mort Hillman" who talks about getting to the DJ sifting through 200 new releases a week, but admitting with a laugh, "Let's say I've got friends in the business. They do me favors." Translation? Payola.

It all comes down to sales and who gets how big a piece of the pie. The article brings up the question of sales and how those numbers were closely guarded even within the industry. It stated, "Even the approximations are wild guesses. Only the label boss knows. He shares his secret with no one." Reading this article, you get the impression that the record business was rife with corruption, and in reality…well, you'll see.

The article quotes a major name, Mercury Records' Art Tallmadge who states plainly, "Without the disc jockey we'd be out of business tomorrow." You had to keep them happy, but you also had to give them a product they weren't afraid to promote. In 1957 there were two names that were spoken in whispers, the two deejays who were kingmakers and had a long list of names to prove it. The number two guy was Ed McKenzie in Detroit, WJBK's "Jack, the Bellboy", and there was no mistake how he felt. If you won "the Bellboy's' favor, you were likely on your way to stardom. If you didn't, he'd leave the mic on and you (and the audience) would hear the record sail across the room into the trash. But the "big dog" was on the south shore of Lake Erie, WERE's Bill Randle.

Randle was the exact opposite of what a disc jockey was trained to do. The one-time high school dropout, who later piled up college degrees and a license to practice law, spoke in a monotone and had an ego as big as any of his artists…whom he probably made into stars anyway. For example, in 1951 Randle told the story of how he and fellow WERE jock Jerry Crocker came upon singer Johnny Ray playing Cleveland's Biscayne Lounge at East 17th and Euclid. They took Ray to Detroit where he signed with Okeh Records, brought him back to Cleveland for a one-nighter at Moe's Main Street and landed Ray a job at $300 a week. Within ten weeks he was pulling down a weekly salary of $3000. Randle had similar stories about breaking Bill Haley, then leading a hillbilly group out of Chester, Pennsylvania, called the Western Aces. The band was promoting a single called "Crazy, Man, Crazy". He booked them at the St. Michaels' Hall in Lorain and after a name change to the Comets the band carved a wide niche in rock and roll history.

Then, of course, there's the legendary appearances by Elvis Presley in Cleveland in October 1955. There was a Friday night concert at Cleveland's Circle Theater, a *Hillbilly Hayride* show promoted by WERE's resident country music aficionado Tommy Edwards with Presley opening for Kitty Wells and Faron Young. Presley didn't draw much interest, sitting alone at a card table in the theater's lobby waiting to be recognized after he did his act. But Randle also had him the next day third on a five-act bill before Bill Haley and Pat Boone at Cleveland's Brooklyn High School. It wasn't just to showcase Presley though it would go down in rock and roll history as the singer's first performance as a rocker north of the Mason-Dixon line. It was also filmed for a Universal Pictures documentary titled, *The Pied Piper of Cleveland: A Day in the Life of a Famous Disc Jockey* (1955) about…. like we have to tell you. Bill Randle. The 47-minute film was shown once and Cleveland deejay Carl Reese, a contemporary of Randle, was in the audience. "Randle didn't like the way it was edited", according to Reese, "and he claimed ownership of the film. He wanted to supervise the edit but didn't want to pay for the work. He thought people should be happy just to work for Bill Randle!" Stories abound about the fate of the film which hasn't been seen since.

Randle famously turned down a request from Presley to manage the singer, and years later regretted that decision when Presley died young in 1977. Both Randle and McKenzie picked the hits based on gut instinct, and so did Chicago's Howard Miller at WIND. Miller, according to the article, pulled down $350,000 in 1957 dollars, so it wasn't likely…if that figure was accurate…. that a label rep could swing him with a couple hundred bucks.

That same article introduced readers to the power of the "artists and repertoire" person or simply the "A & R man", industry reps who would use any means available to them to get certain records played and shape current trends. At the time the king of the A & R guys was a name that would become familiar as a performer and TV star, Mitch Miller. Radio was the way young people with coins in their pocket heard new music so Miller and his kind would focus on the trend setters at key stations. As we'll see, some were more receptive than others, but the article claimed many of the hardline A & R reps just didn't like the product they were pushing.

It quoted RCA Victor's Joe Carlton who expressed serious concern that he was "making hits that people didn't want to hear". Really? Oddly enough, Presley's name comes up. He'd sold 5-million copies of "Don't Be Cruel", and his label rep is quoted as asking (rhetorically), "That means there are 5-million idiots in our country?" Carlton went on to say, "I love teenagers, but I'm pretty tired of having to cater to their adolescent sex responses." As the article continues you sense a distinct bias on behalf of the writers.

The writer goes so far as to say the artists themselves are disgusted by the current product, stating "It's hard to find a single person inside the business who will defend the 'junk music' they pour into your ears from morning to night. Singers sneer at it. Other musicians gripe helplessly over its poor quality. The words 'junk', 'trash', 'moronic', 'depraved', 'asinine', 'creepy', and 'lascivious' pop up again and again in discussions." Let's take a close look at this. If the author of this piece is to be believed he spoke to music industry professionals who intentionally produce and market inferior product and mock the consumers who line their pockets with royalties. The parting shot comes in the final paragraph with a quote from Bally Records' A & R man Lew Douglas lamenting the lack of professional quality in hits of the day, claiming "Sometimes it gets so bad you can't tell a smash hit from a candidate for the garbage can." It concludes with a theory that the music of the day was only sold to teenagers in defiance of their parents.

The article shows photos of Muni, Roberts and Myers above the lurid headline...but that's the only mention they get in the article. It would appear to be an obvious attempt to link local performers to the sensational headline in an attempt to exploit them as "messengers of doom" or at least substandard entertainment. Myers was only on the job for a short time but a rising star, while Muni and Roberts both had loyal followings. The hyper conservative post war media had apparently found a new enemy to publicly demonize, a tactic used successfully by Senators Estes Kefauver when he linked comic books and juvenile delinquency and Senator Joseph McCarthy's wild accusations linking many innocent names to Communism and treason. All would profit in their own way, and the media didn't let up on the debate about the effects of the "devil's jukebox" and the people who delivered the product.

A few months later the Herald Tribune News Service pitted two of New York's most important radio personalities against each other to debate the merits of rock and roll. The piece also ran in the *Akron Beacon Journal*. Alan Freed at WINS was an obvious choice, but he was countered by William B. Williams who was with WNEW, New York's heritage "good music" station, a format that tended to be more sophisticated and meant for an older more relaxed radio audience that favored standards.

Remember that about WNEW.

Freed took a stand that rock and roll was indeed music, "the only real music we can call our own", and Williams agreed it was music but "unfortunately a very narrow and oft times dull repetition of a particular type of music." Then Williams threw down the gauntlet saying, "Ninety percent of the current commercial noise that is passed off as authentic rhythm and blues can only be aptly described as tripe".

Would it last? Freed said the answer was evident, pointing to the record charts showing "55 out of the top 60 best sellers are rock and roll hits. Yes, it will last and for a long time to come!" Williams countered with a thoughtful and rational response suggesting the public would weed out what it thought was worthy predicting "the good beat and contagious rhythm in good palatable rock 'n' roll will have its influence on pop music for a long time. The rest of it will die because of lack of taste." A jab here and there, but a civil exchange with each side standing his ground.

But what about its influence on young listeners? The riot at the Moondog Coronation Ball in Cleveland gave the music an instant reputation and its infamy may well have fueled its popularity and effect on impressionable listeners. Was it an evil influence? Not according to Freed who argued it was exactly the opposite. "When kids have an active interest in something", he claimed, "whether or not it's music, it keeps them from being idle. Keep them interested in something and they don't get into trouble." Maybe. That cast a pretty wide net as to what "interested" young people, though Williams agreed rock and roll could not be defined as an evil medium...while saying certain parties could benefit from the seamier side of the music. It was Williams' contention that, "Many deejays (disc jockeys) are so eager to capitalize on so impressionable a group as teenagers and feed them, day after day, the same kind of musical garbage as so much of rock and roll is. I don't think that any fad like R & R itself contributes to juvenile delinquency. The point is rather that the lack of good standards carries over from mores to music." Could Williams have been referring to Freed and his string of headline grabbing incidents?

The two debated whether the music sold sponsor's products with Freed claiming his listeners bought soft drinks and tickets to movies advertised on his show, while Williams shrugged off those comments saying he heard young expendable cash mostly went to buying singles and smart sponsors saw that. Freed came back saying young people were wise consumers and had a wide range of interests. He cited his own eclectic tastes saying he was a fan of Guy Lombardo both professionally and personally. Williams stressed he was not a fan but plenty of people were and just because he didn't like something didn't make it bad. The two also agreed that jazz on TV would not kill rock and roll. Freed said while he enjoyed that type of music as well as classical, he claimed jazz always had a small audience and record sales showed how poorly it fared against rock and roll. In his response, Williams said music with "merit" would have longevity, and "Perhaps some of the best elements of rock 'n' roll will be refined eventually as good jazz and swing or whatever you want to call it comes to the fore." All in all, an intelligent and well-balanced exchange between two radio industry leaders but, again, as they were with the previous article readers were drawn by a sensational headline that read, "Freed Says Rock Music Good, Williams Labels It Garbage."

While Alan Freed helped define the role of the rock and roll disc jockey and the role music played at that time in the lives of young listeners, Myers was taking it in a new direction as an entertainer. As Ernie Myers pointed out it was in 1957 at WHKK / Akron that Pete Myers was inspired to develop the Mad Daddy, who was later described as "a frantic, neo-Beat disc jockey predisposed to speed-rapping in rhyme." He didn't use the Daddy name at the time but developed his on-air personae using various air names and played so-called "honker" music (with wailing saxophones) and other R & B styles that were familiar to black audiences, some white musicians, and certain groundbreaking disc jockeys like Alan Freed on WJW / Cleveland who presented it on his *Moondog* show and called it rock 'n' roll.

As with Freed in Cleveland, the Akron audience enthusiastically embraced the music as well as the person putting it on the air. Most of the music Myers played originated on all-black record labels that were not pitched to most white disc jockeys because they didn't see an audience for that style of entertainment. Plus, white programmers in the racially segregated fifties picked records like they picked neighborhoods. There was other groundbreaking music out there, like the pioneering sound of southern white rockabilly which Myers also helped to popularize. As one researcher pointed out, these were, "low-budget records that were being cut in music- stores, basements, and the back rooms of diners. He followed his own tastes and eventually introduced a kind of humorous, off-beat rhythm 'n' blues that he called 'wavy gravy."

It would seem evident that Myers had learned to become part of the fabric of entertainment that would test the boundaries of radio to a young audience that willingly accepted something new and far different than the music and radio embraced by their parents' generation. New, different and mom and dad disapproved. That's a big drawing card for the young audience, but the guy working the microphone had a growing base of fans, too.

Myers had one sponsor at WHKK, and that was a vitamin tonic called Black Draft Syrup. Sponsors in Akron were still leery of the new personality, and it was equally puzzling for Myers who expected advertisers to embrace him as quickly as his audience. The Mad Daddy character may have been born the night he vented his desperation by grabbing the microphone and after an impromptu rhyme about his career problems stated, "A fella'd have to be mad, mad, mad … ," to continue that way. His voice fading into echo, it may have been the first time Myers hinted at what would eventually be known as the Mad Daddy.

Pete Myers' historian Jay Hunt suggests the Mad Daddy character may have also been inspired by a number of sources, including Ernie Kovacs, who we mentioned was a favorite of Myers with his characters Auntie Gruesome, Percy Dovetonsils and The Nairobi Trio. The Abbott & Costello horror movies such as *Abbott & Costello Meet Frankenstein* (1948) showed Myers how to use the monster genre in a humorous way. The 1952-53 flying saucer scare captured the imaginations of a good segment of society and made its way into popular culture in pulp magazines, comic books, newspapers and movies. Plus, Myers also used the early bopster jargon of the day like Daddio (Daddy), wavy gravy and mello jello to communicate with his young audience. There were other possible influences, including cartoonist Basil Wolverton's wise-cracking comic strip character *Powerhouse Pepper*, the cutting-edge humor of *Mad* magazine and possibly even the boredom of being a highly creative individual alone at night in a radio station who was willing to take chances to draw an audience. A bigger stage soon called.

In January 1958, Pete Myers took the Mad Daddy to WJW / Cleveland, the former home of Alan Freed and a solid ratings leader among the youth market that was so lucrative to advertisers. It led to some quick shuffling of the WHKK air staff with the station moving its big gun, morning man Garry Miller to Myers' old time slot, and David McLaughlin, from Detroit's WBRB, taking over the *Breakfast Time* show. Mclaughlin had worked at WELL / Battle Creek and WHLS / Port Huron and, like Myers, had some theater on his resume as well. Like Alan Freed before him, Myers was heading to the big 850.

Pete Myers' theme song on WJW-AM, and later on WHK-AM and FM, was *Night Train* by Buddy Morrow. It's a bluesy saxophone driven song, and he followed it with a countdown similar to those in the televised Vanguard rocket launches. Myers also dropped in sounds of screams, hot rods, whistling wind, his own echoey maniacal laugh and other effects into songs. In addition, Myers, like Freed, preferred to play original artists on obscure labels rather than mainstream labels.

Mad Daddy was an immediate hit, much to the chagrin of Ohio Bell the local telephone provider. Within weeks of his debut, Daddy was getting so many calls on the request phones at the North Royalton transmitter studios that it was dangerously jamming the lines. Bell Telephone appealed to WJW management to ask listeners to write their requests on postcards. It did cut down on phone requests, especially when the station's producer just stopped taking many of the calls, but the impact was obvious. It was also stated that other radio stations were already courting Myers, but it was stressed that he was under a strict contract with WJW.

Jay Hunt called this the first of three important phases in Myers' Mad Daddy character, pointing out, "The (WJW) show was more relaxed and easy going. He did everything himself, the show, commercials and in his own voice, station, news and weather breaks. He chose all his own music. The playlists clearly show that few of his songs were popular hits. They tended to be R&B, early rock and roll by obscure artists or songs, unusual instrumentals or novelty records…Myers worked at relating to his teen audience on a personal level. A lot of airtime went to dedications to fans who wrote or phoned in. Every weekend he appeared at high school dances or sock hops around town. A good amount of his influence was passed on by young fans who used Daddy's everyday patter as their own unique style of communication. Writing in Cleveland's *Call & Post* newspaper in a column titled "Echoes from Kennard", junior high journalists Janis Scott and Carol Comer pepper their piece with "daddyisms" including a "scoopie do" preview of the Student Council's upcoming "Top Record Spin" referring to student Marjorie Malcolm being nattily attired in her Mad Daddy boots. While the circumstances regarding the end of his marriage to Sylvia Crane are uncertain, Myers also took the time on March 29th to tie the knot with the second of his three wives, Ann Boyce.

Jim Jaworski was an early and avid fan of Pete Myers and said the distinctive character of the Mad Daddy, along with rarely heard race records marketed to the young generation, deeply concerned many parents. Jaworski says, "If there was anybody in rock and roll for parents to be frightened about, it was Pete Myers, 'Mad Daddy', and there was no question about it. When our generation came along, we were the first generation that didn't have to go off to war. We were the first generation in the history of the world to get our own cars, even though they were junkers and we had to work on them and fix them up. We were the first generation, I believe, to develop our own personal culture. All the other generations had to share their culture with the previous generations. It's what I call the 'split culture.' Rock and roll was uniquely ours, and we really knew that when the parents didn't like it."

Another long time Myers' fan and historian, Greg Miller remembered that era in this way. "You've got to think about what mainstream radio was playing in the 1950s. You had Doris Day and Percy Faith, and rock and roll stations were different. A guy like Pete Myers was very cutting edge, even by today's standards. I think the closest guy that I've heard that even came close was in the WIXY days in the 1960s, when I was a kid. I can remember listening to some of the WIXY deejays…there was the 'Wild Child' and a guy by the name of Jack Armstrong…and they had similar rapid fire 'shouter style' deliveries, and as a kid I used to like to listen to that. You just wanted to hear what they had to say next. They didn't care what they said, and with Mad Daddy, I think it was the same way. You were never quite sure he wasn't going to just launch into some vulgar tirade, or he could just delight you." Miller also pointed to the rare recordings of Myers' program that show "he is always right on the edge…totally unscripted, right off the top of his head...but in perfect syncopation. Everything rhymes, everything is right out there."

Myers as Mad Daddy did breaks, spoke over music beds, and was noted for what was described as his "rhyming scatological style…able to spontaneously create rhymes through an entire four-and-a-half -hour show, doing even commercials in off-the-cuff rhyme at breakneck speed, handling all the physical demands without modern radio conveniences like prerecorded tape machines."

It's also noted that Myers was also creating a bizarre new language. As one Myers' historian stated, "The gabber's fun words appealed to the kid in everyone." Now kids were talking amongst themselves in a new language, Daddy's language, and who knows what they were really saying?

Myers' also referred to his female fans as mellow muffins, and the boys were called ghoul rockers. Hot rodding was a favorite past time among that audience, and race fans were labeled throttle jammers. A recurring song on his show was Andre Williams' *Greasy Chicken* and another favorite was *Ghost Satellite* by Bob & Jerry.

We mentioned Neil McIntyre a bit earlier. He was a teenager who lived in Cleveland Heights and as a student at Heights High was a fan of Pete "Mad Daddy" Myers' show on WJW-AM. He would later say it was the appeal of so-called race records played by black artists that originally drew him in, but the Mad Daddy fascinated him, and he decided to track Myers down. The way he did it was ingenious! He told us, "I had heard the radio station's transmitter was in Seven Hills, so I borrowed my uncle's car and started driving to the west side listening to him on the radio. The closer I got, the signal would come in stronger. All of a sudden, I saw a sign that said WJW. I drove down this dirt road, and there was the transmitter site. That's where he was broadcasting from. So, I knocked on the door, and a guy answers wearing a three piece tweed suit. He said, 'What can I do for you?' and I said, 'I just like your station, and I was wondering if you needed any help.' 'Yeah,' he said, 'Here's a pad and pencil. Write down what the kids say on the phone. They call in requests.' He was by himself, and I sat down to answer phones. At one point, I looked around and saw this guy open the mike, and he turns into 'Mad Daddy!' I couldn't believe it! I thought this fella was an engineer or something like that. He broadcast from the WJW transmitter until he eventually went to WHK-AM." At that same time McIntyre saw Myers' genius at improv firsthand. McIntyre claimed he would hand Myers a handful of dedication slips and Myers would make rhymes with them as he read them cold on-the-air, and never used notes. Plus, he fired them off like a machine gun and never repeated the crazy rhymes.

Myers' brother, Ernie, would say, "Kids sure appreciated him!." While he played rhythm and blues almost exclusively, Ernie stressed "It was not his type of music, but it fit the character. They got mail (in Cleveland) stating, 'What are you trying to do? Pollute kids' minds?" The kids seemed to say, "Pollute away!"

It's been said that the best advertising is word of mouth, and word got around quickly about the Mad Daddy. Jim Jaworski said the unlimited accessibility of rock and roll radio while riding in your own car helped solidify teenagers' loyalty not only to the music but to "Mad Daddy" as well. "You had six buttons on the car radio back then. With those buttons on the radio, you knew every station was on the right channel, and you'd hit those buttons and you knew what you would hear. Myers wasn't on for two weeks before everybody in Cleveland knew about him. I had told one of my friends here about ten years ago, 'You know. Way back then we never used to watch television. You know why? Because we were more interested than what was on television. You could go to any drive-in restaurant and hear fifty cars in the back lot all with Mad Daddy on the radio. You could hear it for four – five blocks away."

Greg Miller also observed that the music was a key component of Mad Daddy's appeal. Myers played music that was as distinctive as his delivery and alter-ego. "There's absolutely no comparison to what he was playing and what the other disc jockeys were playing. Bill Randle was a big radio deejay in Cleveland. The other big names were Carl Reese, who spun rock and roll records. 'Mad Daddy' was not playing Frankie Avalon. 'Mad Daddy' wasn't even playing Duane Eddy. The stuff he was playing was absolutely cutting edge, records that were probably closer to what we would consider a form of punk rock today, or alternative rock. But he spun it in such a way that it was a real free flow. I think the show was bigger than the music. The audience was not listening so much for the songs. 'Mad Daddy' would not have played even the Everly Brothers. He was playing stuff that was different."

McIntyre agreed, but he doesn't buy the argument that part of Myers' popularity came from airing race records which drew so much attention to Alan Freed just a few years before on that same station. McIntyre believed, "Parents didn't really pay attention to what their kids were listening to because they would be in their rooms lying in bed at night with their transistor radios under their pillows. Cars, too. They weren't listening with their families, so their families didn't know what they were listening to. They would know if the kid bought the record and brought it home and played it and all of a sudden, they would say, 'What is that music you're playing?' and everything else. To them, their teenagers were listening to songs, but they had no idea what they were listening to."

Back to Jaworski. He stated that the music was a huge draw, but adds it was Myers who was still the center of attention. Jaworski observed, "The hours that he wasn't on the air you could get the other music. That was twenty hours a day. We had plenty of hours to listen to regular music. There were only four hours a day when he came on and you'd better listen to him because you didn't know what you were going to miss."

Miller points out, "You were listening to Pete Myers the way people would listen to Howard Stern today. You never knew what was going to come out of his mouth next. You were on the edge and just hoping…was he going to step over the line and say something just totally off the wall. When you listen to him on the recordings today it has a hypnotic effect! Plus, the sound effects in the show were terrific. There was a bubbling cauldron, and he used a lot of reverb on his voice."

Myers' unique scatological on-air patter was being refined during his years at WJW. In one of the rare recordings that exists of Myers' air work, we hear in his show on April 1, 1958 that he was able to link his own catch phrases in a common theme of disc jockey patter, though he may have reached a bit by referring to WJW's 850 on the dial as "Radio 85." Listeners heard:

"Here you are in the land of glee. Floppin' and boppin' at 10:03."

You know exactly where you are. Tuned to radio 85 on your wavy gravy jar.

Tell those bubbles of oobladi what kind of record this jukebox is going to be."

Later that same evening, Myers lost no energy as he led into dedications from his station fan mail, stating:

Ooba dooba, Scooby doo. 26 before 11 the time in rhyme in R & B heaven.

In our first hour of power as on we go with our head all aglow.

The winky blinky light is glowing just right tonight as we got mail by the bale.

Remember we giggle, we jiggle, we bop and blast.

Mail, mail, mail keeps the show on the air to make it last.

Remember, never chicken…we're always stickin' so we gotta read all these names and burst into flames."

Assisted by Neil McIntyre, Myers would then read names off pieces of paper rhyming at a fast pace off the top of his head until his next record and dropping the slips to the floor.

A good part of the business of radio was to sell records. Ratings and revenue keep stations on the air, and personalities sell the product to a target audience. The WHK disc jockeys at the time tied in with local record stores for a unique method of driving traffic to the stores while promoting the station. It was called a "Half Price Pick". Each of the WHK jocks would choose a record every week and listeners could pick it up for fifty cents if they used a "secret password" from the deejays. It impressed radio host Bill Gavin who was with the syndicated *Lucky Lager Dance Time* telling Billboard, "When Pete (Myers) picked 'Whole Lotta Lovin', kids went out in a pelting rain to get the bargain. That's loyalty." That same sales gimmick had success in other radio markets across the U.S. Myers also had a thought of selling a record of his own.

A few years before, in July 1956, Bill Buchanan and Dickie Goodman released their novelty record *The Flying Saucer* and it spawned a series of other comedy recordings. Eager to capitalize on that trend, Pete Myers released two comedy recordings as "The Joker" on the Cleveland based G & F Records. The A-side, "I Love a Practical Joke*"*, describes a battle of dangerous practical jokes between Myers and his friend, Melvin, using cobras, misguided diesel trucks into a home, nitroglycerin, a kidnapped lion from the zoo, high tension wires from a railroad track, and poison gas resulting in Myers death as he gasps with his dying breath, "I love a practical joke!" While it was released under the name "The Joker", the piece ends with Myers' familiar maniacal laugh. The commentary is delivered to a bongo beat.

The B-side, "What is a Fisteris*?"*, was basically a straight commentary on a nonsensical question stating, among others, that a fisteris is "big as a grendel, tiny as a suzman and sometimes middle sized like a fremesis on nibbling on the freeze." It mixes strange rhymes with made up words accompanied by an instrumental version of the Chuck Berry composition "In the Wee, Wee Hours". At two minutes and twenty-nine seconds into the recording Myers' voice is heard in a backwards message that would later be revealed as "If I said this in English I could turn this radio station into a parking lot." The song includes a blues piano / bass / guitar / drum combo background.

Myers also won a spot on WJW's television sister station, debuting on April 12, 1958, as host of WJW-TV's double feature horror movie program. The first offering at 11:20 p.m. was *Dracula* (1931*)* followed by *Chamber of Horrors* (1940) , with the Mad Daddy appearing before and after commercials. Keep in mind that TV was still in its early years and the technology that put it on-the-air was oversized and extremely heavy. Myers argued unsuccessfully to have a camera suspended upside down from the studio ceiling, which would have been impossible due to its weight. Instead, Myers did the show in full Mad Daddy regalia hanging upside down from a pole. The show failed to catch on and was canceled after just four weeks. Oddly enough, because of atmospheric conditions and a lack of competing signals on that wavelength, the Mad Daddy TV show actually "bounced" into Canada!

As Myers' popularity grew, so did the demand for personal appearances. As Mcintyre told us, record hops were a very busy and profitable time for Myers and his promotional team who would set up several appearances per night. "We would tell the promoters that Pete wouldn't appear until the 'mood was right.' First, he would come out in some type of Kabuki type make-up, white face make-up with a black cape, and then we set the mood with these heavy r & b songs. I remember one of the hops was in Ada, Ohio. It had a population of like 950. They packed the gymnasium. People came from all over the place, and this was a fairly rural area. I could remember doing shows like that and while Pete was doing 'Mad Daddy,' his wife would be at another place setting up for another hop the same night. We would do two record hops a night, and after he left for the other appearance, I would shut down the first. I could remember doing a prom hop for a graduating class, going to another right after and getting home at about 2:30 in the morning… Pete was a total entertainer, and even though we didn't bring the sound effects or the stuff from the studio, we would give out records the kids loved that Pete used on his show. They might not have been popular on other stations, like *The Greasy Chicken*, but Pete's fans wanted to hear them."

While Myers made huge inroads in the Cleveland market, Alan Freed was returning to the Rubber City that April with a jaw dropping lineup of future Rock and Roll Hall of Famers. He promised "1958's Biggest All-Star Show at the Akron Armory hosted by "the King of Rock and Roll Akron's own Alan Freed". This is significant because despite his defection to Cleveland's WJW, the Moondog Ball debacle, his exit to New York City and his fight to break down entertainment (and society's) racial barriers, Freed was embraced by fans in his old hometown. It should also be noted that the Armory show was scheduled for a Wednesday with an afternoon matinee at 4:30 just in time for the after-school crowd. How's this for a concert lineup? JoAnn Campbell starts the ball rolling, doo-wop with the Pastels followed by Cleveland's "Screamin' Jay" Hawkins, the Larry Williams Orchestra followed by the top selling Dicky Doo and the Don'ts and the groundbreaking all girl group from the Bronx, the Chantels. Then Billy Ford did double duty with his own group the Thunderbirds and as a duet with Lillie Bryant as, "Lillie and Billy". Plenty more to come with Danny and the Juniors, the Diamonds and Frankie Lymon, with Chuck, Berry, Buddy Holly and the Crickets and headliner Jerry Lee Lewis rounding off the bill. That same tour visited Canton's Memorial Auditorium with many of the same acts along with Danny and the Juniors and Freed's orchestra featuring Sam Taylor. "Alan Freed's Big Beat" tour lived up to its name.

He'd only been in Cleveland for a short time, but Myers was impatient and by spring 1958, he was said to be frustrated that the Mad Daddy character was not bigger than it already was and thought a station change could be the answer. An offer came from WHK-AM and FM (or, as Mad Daddy would say, "Amm and Fum. Don't be dumb!") WHK offered to double his salary, but there was a major stumbling block. Columnist George Condon caught wind of the change and wrote in his *Plain Dealer* column in mid-May that Myers was about to abandon the WJW ship. He pointed out Mad Daddy's huge following among younger listeners that he won with his, "use of rhyme and occasional macabre laugh", and included Myer's hosting role on sister TV station WJW's Saturday night double-feature horror films. That job was over as soon as he left the WJW radio gig, though Myers was not all that happy with TV anyway. Condon called Myers hiring the first official act by WHK's new owners, the Dumont Broadcasting Corporation which was set to take over WHK on June 1 of that year. One little problem. Okay, a big problem.

Myers contract with WJW had a 90-day guaranteed non-compete clause, meaning he would still be paid but could not work at another station for three months. The contract also stated Myers would have to give WJW a 90-day notice, which he failed to do. As a result, he was kept off the air at a critical time in his career when he needed to maintain a high profile. His replacement at WJW was a young disc jockey from Detroit named Casey Kasem, who would go on to a nationally recognized career in radio, television and commercial voiceover. To Kasem's credit, he was a great radio entertainer, but there was only one Mad Daddy.

Condon wrote in his column just a few days after his initial speculation, and Myers' official departure that an "erstwhile WJW star disk jockey will be an idle laddy for the next three months. All branches of station WJW, AM, FM and TV, apparently are displeased with his announced decision to quit and join the WHK staff. He was immediately dropped from the WJW radio schedule" and "WJW also dropped the mad sire as host of its Saturday night horror double-feature, not – however, not without admission that mad daddies are not easily replaced. The horrible fact is that WJW-TV will go along on Saturday nights without any kind of a horror host and plans to modify its double bill to half horror. The second feature film will be horrible, by official designation. The early movie will be a regular, non-spook affair and any viewer who gets frightened will be strictly on their own." The controversy was far from over and lingers today.

Again, while his exit had been strongly hinted at in the press, and followed through as predicted, Jay Hunt still questioned his quick departure from WJW suggesting Myers' may have been pushed out or forced the station's hand with an off-color comment. The comment, which has been repeated by almost every Myers' fan, was "Hang loose Mother Goose! Dipped her rag in tomato juice!", which some saw as a crude reference to menstruation. Hunt stated, "I am convinced that his sudden departure from WJW was a result of the rumored 'tomato juice' incident. I remember listening to him one night and the next he was gone with no farewell or explanation of any kind. I suspect it really happened on his last WJW show, that the FCC suspended him, and he was fired. The press releases about contract difficulties were just a cover. The long-standing rumors of the 'tomato juice' incident have bothered me for years. Based on my own memory and surrounding known facts, I now believe I have finally put the pieces together."

Hunt recalled that on Tuesday, June 2, 1958, the Mad Daddy show had simply disappeared with no explanation from WJW as to why, and he later learned of his move to WHK. While no tape is known to exist to prove this, Hunt is convinced beyond a doubt that, having signed a new deal with WHK and being told by WJW management that they would enforce the 90 day non-compete clause in his contract, Pete decided to show his displeasure and get even with the station. Hunt also believes that is why he signed off his June 1, 1958, show with the following poem:

Hang loose, Mother Goose
Dipped her rag in tomato juice
Goodbye, Mad Daddy, Goodbye!

Hunt went on to say, "He hoped that this would anger WJW management and perhaps even get them in trouble with the FCC. He figured that being so late at night it would not have been heard by most of his young fans, or even understood by those who did happen to hear it so his reputation would not be damaged." Years later, columnist D. L. Stewart called the alleged comments, "a little piece of doggerel that was interpreted by some as poetic references to menstrual cycles."

Hunt also claimed this event definitely did not take place on WHK on June 29, 1959, as it has sometimes been reported, saying he listened to Mad Daddy's last show on June 26, 1959 and tuned in to WHK again the following Monday, June 29 just in case. As Hunt recalled, "He was gone and, much to my disappointment, replaced by a 'middle of the road' show. So I know for a fact there was no Mad Daddy show on Monday, June 29, 1959. I guess we will never have conclusive evidence, but this is the only explanation that makes sense, given that I personally heard both the June 2, 1958, and June 29, 1959 non-appearances."

Whatever the reason, Myers found himself banned from broadcasting at a time when keeping a high profile was critical to his career.

Chapter Three

"Is it Music or Garbage?"

Pete Myers kept the Mad Daddy personae in front of the public as best he could during his forced contract hiatus. Weekends were golden time for Northeast Ohio's young people, and he would sometimes do three or four stage show appearances a day at movie theaters showing horror films. Myers had started making appearances during and after his short stint as a late-night movie host on WJW-TV, and his non-compete status did not include stage shows. A recently discovered promotional film for his theater appearances promises two hours of *Mad Daddy's Shock Theater* with swamp spiders and jungle worms lurking in the audience. The clip also challenges young women to see if their date is a man or a mouse, and states, "Girls, here's a chance to cuddle up with your dates!" The promotional clip goes on to say "It" would be on stage and urges patrons to buy their tickets early because of a sure sell-out with no standing room access. Trailers for the movies scheduled to be shown would be spliced into the promo, including double features such as *Invasion of the Saucer Men* (1957*)* and, *I Was a Teenage Frankenstein* (1957), *I Was a Teenage Werewolf* (1957) and *The Screaming Skull* (1958), among others. While the appearances were wildly successful and profitable, Myers was not reaching the audiences he could with radio.

Myers could well support himself. He was still receiving a salary but was barred from doing radio for the remainder of his 90-day agreement. He was said to be extremely concerned and came to the conclusion that he would have to do something both daring and newsworthy to stay in the eye of the mass audience. In addition, Myers had gotten remarried that April, and was anxious to progress with his professional and personal life.

There were plenty of changes afoot at WHK besides hiring Myers who was yet to crack the mic. Station manager Henry W.

(Bud) Simmen announced the station would sever ties with the NBC radio network that July and the next logical place for the net would be Myers old radio home at WJW. Simmen also announced additional staff changes at WHK once Metropolitan Broadcasting Company took over management duties. It was expected they would be importing on-air talent from outside the state. But the talent they hired from "across the street" was about to announce a defining moment in his career and Cleveland radio history.

Myers came up with an idea to fill a portion of Lake Erie with Jello gelatin and parachute into the lake wearing a Zorro costume to promote the Walt Disney TV series of the same name. It would be a tough sell. He petitioned the Civil Aeronautics Administration for permission to jump 3000 feet from a Piper Cub airplane, hinting that Disney Productions would sponsor the event if he also dropped hundreds of promotional copies of the "Theme from Zorro" song (Disneyland Records F-062) by singer Henry Calvin. The Coast Guard was consulted, and Commander E.R. Henry warned Myers that the relative shallowness of Lake Erie produced choppy waves and could be extremely dangerous. In fact, the odds of survival might only be 50-50 for an experienced parachutist. Just hours before Myers scheduled jump he confided to producer Neil McIntyre that his "extensive experience" was one jump over North Korea while in the service. Tension was mounting over a promotion that might be described as foolhardy at best.

This is a stunt that would likely be rejected flat out today, but the 1950s were a different time. The Cleveland chapter of the Parachute Club of America was brought in to offer Myers additional instruction in safety techniques as well as a skin diver to rescue him if his chutes tangled on the way down. The club also stressed the extreme danger in the jump with the group's board chairman Willis Downing warning that a chutist jumping into the water would not be able to inflate his life jacket until he was free of his harnesses. Downing was a former paratrooper and emphasized that it was not an easy technique to learn. His club was obligated to help, but he also made it clear to the press that he didn't like the idea one bit. He told reporters "Our group has the best safety record of any PCA chapter. If anything happened to Myers it would reflect badly on us."

The Parachute Club also expressed additional concerns about his safety in a water landing. Myers was eager to stage the stunt, and again falsely claimed he'd parachuted hundreds of times in Korea. He stressed their worries were unfounded and his experience would keep him perfectly safe. In reality, if they'd known Myers had only jumped from a plane once it is almost certain the Coast Guard and CAA would have denied him permission if they had known the truth. The skin diver assigned to the press boat that would retrieve Myers after the jump was equipped with an aqualung expecting to rescue him from under the waves.

There are few serious interviews with Myers out of character regarding his time as Mad Daddy. In 1967, WZAK disc jockey Dick Liberatore conducted a phone interview with Myers and asked him why he would pursue such a dangerous stunt. Myers said, "Why did I do it? That was a warm summer! To be very frank with you, I never thought I would have to do it. I told one of the columnists out there… that I'd asked the boss at WJW to let me out of my contract and he told me to go jump in the lake. I said I would, and somebody put it in the paper, and it just snowballed and one day I was out there with two parachutes and I had to do it!"

There were certain restrictions. The CAA put its foot down on his plans to wear a caped costume over the chute and refused to allow him to distribute records from the air. Plus, Myers failed to locate enough Jello to fill a contained portion of the inner harbor, and even if he did it's unlikely the agencies would have allowed him to dump it in the lake. That didn't stop the promotion. A week before the jump word of mouth alerted fans about the stunt and Myers was committed to following through.

The inherent danger wasn't lost on WHK management, but there was still an opportunity to ease the tense moments with a smile. When station manager Simmen was asked if he was interested in a "radio first" by joining Myers in his jump he responded, "It is a tempting idea and the picture of Myers and me drifting through the air, hand in hand, is a fascinating one – but I think I'll pass it up anyway."

It drew about 300 fans, and at 3 p.m. on June 14, 1958, Myers climbed into his friend's plane and buzzed the crowd before stepping out for the jump. As Myers remembered, "Once the parachute opened up it was all right because that's the big suspense. The first three or four seconds... because that first step is terrible!" Producer Neil Mcintyre, Myers' wife Ann and his agent, Ray Goodlander watched from a cabin cruiser as he yelled "Zorro!" and jumped from the plane for an estimated 100 second fall into the choppy waves below. The water was cold, about 60 degrees, and Myers was pulled from the lake to resounding cheers. Myers dried off on the boat, put on his Mad Daddy cape, and upon reaching shore cornered *Cleveland News* reporter Jan Mellow to say he'd written a poem while still in the air over Lake Erie. He told the reporter, "If you want mellow publicity, bail out and win it. Though Mad Daddy's not on the air, hang loose Mother Goose...he's in it!" He added the, "fifty-fifty odds were better than I get at Hialeah [race track]" adding, "I didn't want those cats to forget me." Myers then waded into the crowd of admirers to sign autographs and pose for photos before heading to the nearby Captain Frank's Restaurant on the East Ninth Street pier to warm up with hot coffee. When asked what he might do next for publicity until he was allowed back on-the-air, Myers said, "Somebody suggested something about setting off sticks of dynamite in each of my ears...but I don't want to do anything foolhardy!" Years later, in the 1967 interview, Myers was asked if he was afraid once he was in the air and would have to follow through. His only response was, "Any fears? Like I said that first step is a big one."

Myers' "heroics" didn't escape the national press. *Billboard*'s June Bundy noted that a lot of stations were staging high profile stunts with one station even giving away what they claimed were replicas of Elvis Presley's Army dog tags, another paying a family's rent, food and utilities for a month and yet another offering car payments. Myers' future home at WNEW had a young woman calling herself "Miss Portable Radio" walking the neighborhoods in New York and Westchester with a radio next to her ear and spotters calling the station to give her location. Across the country stations offered dates with major stars, free albums (which at the time were pricey), and one even had a $100 prize to the listener who guessed the exact time to the minute when a local employer would officially end a labor dispute with its striking workers. There were treasure and scavenger hunts and even a contest to determine what a "Purple People Eater" as celebrated in song would look like. There were glaring differences between what the stations were hoping to accomplish and Myers' plans. The Mad Daddy was between jobs and calling attention to himself. During his jump he would toss out empty record sleeves for the Chordettes' "Zorro" and folks who retrieved them would get the record by visiting WHK. The other jocks at the station were already plugging the record on a regular basis. One other major difference between Myers and other station promotion and that was no one was putting their life in peril. Bundy commended Myers' "promotional valor" …but wondered if he planned to follow through on such a highly risky stunt. Word got around quick after he did.

Just a few days later the jump was still in the news. George Condon wrote in his column about the importance of accurate time checks on radio. He wrote, "They dropped 'Mad Daddy' Pete Myers into Lake Erie the other day and he came out telling the time just as if nothing at all had happened, except maybe a little water in the ears, which is an advantage to a fellow who has to play to rock 'n' roll all day."

Anxious to see what he might try next, newspapers reported on July 8 that Myers planned to broadcast his first day on WHK on August 1 from a huge bucket of Jello. Again, there was a snag when Myers reportedly couldn't find a tank with refrigeration coils big enough to handle 100 gallons of the gelatin, though he planned to contact the makers of the dessert to ask their help in locating one. Myers also took the role of Steve in the Musicarnival summer tent production of *Show Boat* that month for a two-week run. On July 30 he was honored by Fillippo's Restaurant at 12909 Miles Avenue in Cleveland when it debuted Mad Daddy Giggle Juice named after Myers in anticipation of his move to WHK.

Chapter Four

Hanging from the Ceiling!

Myers next stop was the WHK studios near East 55th and Euclid Avenue. This begins what Jay Hunt believes was the second and most productive phase of Pete Myers' career as Mad Daddy, stating, "His appearance on WHK was much more of a planned and commercialized format. He no longer did his own station breaks. Johnny Walter or other announcers did them. The Mad Daddy persona was ramped up a notch being faster paced and much more frenetic. He now appeared in Dracula costume at his public events, and introduced his famous opening and closing themes, "Night Train" and "In the Dark". The Mad Daddy show faced some stiff competition in the 8 p.m. time slot from Ray Otis at Myers' old station WJW and Phil McLean on WERE, both powerhouse personalities. At the same time, the highly popular Johnny Walters was Myers' lead in show and the Mad Daddy was at WHK because of the damage he did to other stations across the dial.

Hunt pointed out that much less time was given to dedications, and there were many more commercials, one after every two songs. Plus, advertising was targeted to his teen audience, soda pop, blemish creams, razors, 'going steady' rings, Batty Bucks (shoes), speedway races etc. Often the commercials were made-up by Pete himself and all were delivered in the Mad Daddy personae. The show featured more popular hit songs in addition to his own favorites.

While he kept up a busy schedule both on and off the air, it was Mad Daddy that was getting the attention and not Pete Myers. Producer McIntyre noted that's exactly the way he wanted it. He stated that the real Pete Myers was pretty much a mystery even to those in his inner circle saying, "He was like many performers. Myers had one personality on the radio and was a completely different person when he was off. Very quiet. After I had known him for a while, we sat in a bar for a few hours having drinks and I don't remember having a real conversation with him. Off the air he was a person of few words. When he was working, he was all words! His hobby was his work. I got to know him fairly well, at WJW and when I followed him to WHK."

Myers was also loyal to his friends with McIntyre saying, "At WJW I was a volunteer, but when he went to WHK Myers told the management I was the guy who pretty much picked his music, and they made me the music director."

The publicity worked. The Mad Daddy fan base grew dramatically, and while he was still courted by small record labels to play their product, nationally known artists and producers were knocking on his door as well. The manufacturers of Double Cola hired him on to do a national ad that appeared on *American Bandstand* (1958), and his appearances at amusement parks, record stores and other retail outlets drew huge crowds. He would drive up in his pink Pontiac draped in his black Dracula cape and would have the audience in the palm of his hand. A recording of the Mad Daddy show on WHK shows he had lost none of his bravado or talent for off-beat scatological rhyme. With a suspense music bed underneath, Mad Daddy was heard saying:

"Loopin' and a scoopin' and a rockin' and reelin'.

This is Mad Daddy here and we're hangin from the ceiling!

Now, I know the show is nutty but it's never ever dull.

Not as long as the liiiiiiight burns bright in my skull."

One of Mad Daddy's on-air trademarks was something he called Zoomerating. It was a spontaneous rapid-fire recitation of nonsensical words in alphabetical order, sometimes in reverse, describing his show. He never did it the same way twice, and it became one of the most distinctive bits on the Mad Daddy show. Here's an example from his show of July 26, 1958:

"Bumpa dumpa jing jing, On we go. This is Mad Daddy on my final show. But don't tune out 'cause we're not through yet. We haven't done my alphabet! Here we go, let's scare them to death.

                                                                          Mad Daddy

From A to Z all in one big breath! (Deep intake of breath.) Aviating, bobbalating, crashevading, danceapating, elevating, fanagating, groovygating, hoopalating, idolating, jigglating, koolaidabating, lollypoparating, mutating, noisemaking, oobladobedating, poopaquating, quaking, raking, shaking, taking, ubulating, vegelating, wigglating, x-rating, yoyorating and zoomerating.

Still got breath to say…. you're tuned in here to WHK!"

Greg Miller likened Mad Daddy's show to an audio tapestry. He noted,

"It was really just Pete Myers and an assistant in production. They did everything with very primitive equipment. He had a reverb effect. He had some sound effects. But they did that show live. The sound effects that were introduced and the timing was done by cueing the sound engineer and that was it. For him to come up with fresh material for a four hour show every night and keep it fresh and cutting edge, he must have been a caffeine machine. It was just hypnotic. The guy had such a rapid fire and unique delivery. It's almost like poetry. His delivery was so inspired. It was frenetic, but poetic."

Miller also pointed to another factor that made the show unique and that was Myers' taste in music, pointing out that it was extremely cutting edge, and even beyond rock and roll. "I looked at some of his play lists, the stuff he was playing at the station. Al Elias' "King Kong", the Rockefellers' "Orange Peel", Mickey Hawks' "Bip Bop Boom", Andre Williams from Detroit with "The Greasy 'Chicken". There are only a few of these that are even remembered let alone played any more. He would use Buddy Morrow's "Night Train" as an intro, more of a jazz piece, and he had a real sense for what blended and what didn't. It was a free flow, stream of consciousness type thing in his head and he was sound tracking it himself. He was a real artist.

Myers could maintain Mad Daddy's top speed energy level from the first notes of his theme music to his sign off. On the recording of his June 25, 1959, show we hear:

Yeah, the bubbles are cooling and we gotta go.

We're coming to the end of another show.

Brook Benton, and *I Want To Thank You, Baby*. It's going to be really big.

It sends crazy, wavy purple and orange spots under your Daddy's wig!

It's flying out time, but before we do one final word here about the Rendezvous.

With the pop and the bop and the rhythm and the blue, those rock and roll records are stacked up for you at 300 Prospect Avenue.

Listen to your Daddy and take his advice.

Get my crazy wavy feature record tomorrow just half price!

It's your really big chance to save lots of money, and still build up a big collection honey.

Fall by tomorrow and be sure to say, Daddy sent me in from WHK!

What was surprising was despite Pete Myers' aversion to one-on-one contact, he welcomed meeting crowds of fans as the Mad Daddy. Many of those fans would listen to the shows in their cars and eventually make their way down to the WHK studios at 5000 Euclid Avenue. After his show, Myers would emerge from the studio for a few seconds dressed in a long flowing Dracula cape with his face highlighted with grease paint make-up. He would sign autographs, pose for photographs and then exit with a flourish and a maniacal laugh through a back door, speeding out of the parking lot in his pink Pontiac. Jaworski remembered other appearances. "I saw him at the Berea Fairgrounds in (August) 1958. He came to the Berea fair. WHK had a tent there. They brought him in at that time, and they had police all over the place. They had to escort him in with the police, and later escort him out. If you listened to the tapes and imagine what he was like, that was what he was like in person. He was absolutely wild. We knew as kids right away….kids are pretty sharp…we knew right away that this guy was really something very unique."

More from Jaworski. "The tent was packed. He had the cape, and the unique thing about the cape was that it had the hood, and he would ride around Cleveland in what I believe was a pink '58 Pontiac convertible with that bat cape on…At the end of his radio show (on WHK) in downtown Cleveland, he would go outside and there would be a mob out there waiting for him. They were his people."

WHK announcer Ernie Anderson was Myers' lead-in twice a day in split shifts at WHK, starting from noon to 2 p.m. when Myers would do the afternoon shift until 4 p.m., and then from 6 to 8 p.m., when Myers would return as Mad Daddy until 10 p.m. While Anderson questioned Myers' tactics to gain attention, there's little doubt that Myers greatly influenced Anderson's portrayal of "Ghoulardi" on WJW-TV's *Shock Theater* (1963-66) with use of weird sound effects, beatnik patter, and strange lingo. Ghoulardi was an extension of Ernie Anderson's bizarre sense of humor, but there is little doubt he was influenced by Myers even borrowing the term "Amrap", which was Parma spelled backwards. Parma is a west side suburb of Cleveland with a heavy ethnic Polish population. Anderson also had plenty of opportunities to see the Myers magic firsthand. After his first two hours on the air, Myers would hand the show over to Anderson for an hour of news and features and after his dinner break (reportedly two or more martinis) BAM! The door kicked open for an evening of Mad Daddy!

Other WHK staff members remembered Myers as well. Johnny Holliday called Myers the "oddest of (his) fellow radio jocks, as well as the most talented and intriguing." When Myers was on-the-air in the imaginary Dracula Hall he drew the blinds and kept the door closed and no one was allowed entry during his show. There was a strict policy of no visitors and only his personal soundman Arnie Rosenberg was privy to what went on in the studio. Rosenberg said Myers act was completely spontaneous, and he was often hard pressed to keep up with Mad Daddy. Eventually Myers would allow an outsider into the studio, but those occasions were few and far between

Holliday would write in his memoirs that he was a bit intimidated by Myers' style and brilliance, claiming his "Jekyll and Hyde" persona made him somewhat unapproachable. While he was polite and cordial, he was close to very few, and Holliday felt he simply lived in a different world than everyone else.

Myers' brother, Ernie, recalled he once did an unscheduled live simulcast with Pete as the Mad Daddy between San Diego and Cleveland Pete Myers called Ernie while he was on the air at KOGO / San Diego to say "hello" and did the Mad Daddy. Ernie Myers recalls Pete got a tremendous response similar to his fans in Cleveland. Daddy's fans in Cleveland were legion and, in one particular case, potentially rabid. As Halloween neared in 1958 Myers arrived at work one day to find a package addressed to him with a live bat! No photos exist of the new pet but word got out to the local papers that Myers found it a new home in his studio.

Myers' rapid-fire delivery was only one aspect of his appeal. He also had a tight command of the studio and became a technological wizard with the primitive equipment of the time. Former disc jockey Norm N. Nite was one of the very few privileged individuals to actually see Myers at work in the studio at his prime. "I was a fan, of course, like most people living in Cleveland at that particular time of the 1950s, listening to his show religiously two hours a night Monday through Friday. I became very very fascinated by what he was doing, and I remember going down to WHK and walking into the studio on 50th and Euclid and watching him do his show when he had the two long things with turntables, four on each side. He was doing that show with turntables and discs and everything, when nowadays it's so much easier to do a show and the records are two minutes in length. It was just fascinating to watch him work."

As 1958 gave way to a new year, *Plain Dealer* columnist George Condon reviewed the events of the previous twelve months. Cleveland was a much bigger media market at the time with mega talents and huge media names like Bill Randle, Bill Gordon, Dorothy Fuldheim and others. Even so, Mad Daddy's name figured prominently for his work in and out of the studio.

A look at the daily radio listings also revealed an interesting change. In his early days at WHK Myers was listed in all day parts with his given name and Mad Daddy attached to his name at 8 p.m., but in spring 1959 it was Myers at 6 and Daddy at 8 as if they were two different people. Granted, two different on-air personae, but this was the same station that just a few months before showed Myers and Daddy both in newspaper ads as the same person. The ad read, "Have you heard this one!", next to a photo of a cowled Mad Daddy followed underneath with a picture of Myers stating, "Pete Myers, alias 'Mad Daddy' one of WHK's 'Five with Flair'." Myers time slot was listed as 2-4 p.m. with Daddy doing six days Monday through Saturday from 8-10 p.m. The bottom of the ad states the WHK mission with "Hear the loveliest, liveliest sound in town, all day on WHK 1420 on your radio dial." This may well have been an attempt to warn the public that Daddy was for specific tastes other than the soft sounds of the daytime format.

Along with his on-air schedule and live appearances, Pete Myers branched out into marketing himself on the retail level. Nite recalled attaching the Mad Daddy name to a product or retail outlet would bring dramatic results. Appearances were key to his appeal. "He knew how to promote himself, because if someone sponsored his show like Record Rendezvous...'at the 'vous! All the round sounds and nothing square!' Green's Jewelers and all the things he would promote. Horne's on 71st and Carnegie. People just loved him because he was so good at getting that name identification with the product. He knew how to sell."

Greg Miller pointed out, "If you look at the advertisements, it looks like on the weekends he was promoting himself at record hops somewhere, and the big buzz would be 'Mad Daddy is going to make an appearance' and give away some records or something. Or the county fair, or there would be the opening of a store, a supermarket somewhere. He would promote it on the show and make an appearance."

Jim Jaworski added, "He had the 'Batty Bucks.' Stone Shoes in Cleveland had made up a special set of shoes with bat wings on them. The kids would go out and buy these 'Batty Bucks', and he took everything by storm."

Myers' show of June 26, 1959, provides a glimpse at the way Mad Daddy would market his own brand of footwear that was introduced the previous year at the Stone's Shoe store chain. "We're all just bubbly in the land of rhyme, and it's time to make a buck cause it's commercial time. If you like Daddy's rhythm and blues, you'd better stop by Stone's and get those shoes. Remember, in style and value and fit you get more at any neighborhood Stone's shoe store. You find them everywhere. Southland, Westgate and Shaker Square. Downtown? You can buy them there at Ninth and Euclid.

Remember, half the fun of having feet is wearing romper stompers that look this neat. $6.95 for girls. $9.95 for boys. That's batty bucks we're talking about. Styles for everybody...the kind that everyone enjoys ...at Stone's. You'll find those batty bucks really big with Mad Daddy wings that will flip your wig! For dancing on the ceiling there's a non-skid sole. It's the official foot gear for rock and roll. Yes sir! You'll be really digging Akron or Barberton or Orange or Heights High if you wear my shoes when you go bye-bye!"

Myers participation in a promotion meant more revenue flow into WHK and the station would advertise his appearances with a station wagon fitted with large bullhorn speakers on its roof and signs on each side of the vehicle. But nothing sold the appearance like Mad Daddy himself talking up the event on his show. Again, we refer to the show of June 25 as he plugs his sponsor, Record Rendezvous.

"Whippy dippy do dow. Scooby doo! Before we play another etch now here's a word from the 'vous. At 300 Prospect Avenue.

They got the pop and the bop and the rhythm and the blue. And the monoraul records and the stereo, too! They're all racked up and they're waiting for you. 300 Prospect Avenue! I'm sure you're gonna whip in and say, "Daddy sent me in from WHK!" Round sounds, none of the square.

The Rendezvous sonny…buy your records there!"

It should be noted that the Record Rendezvous chain and its main store at 300 Prospect Avenue were owned by Leo Mintz, who sponsored and supplied records for Alan Freed's groundbreaking Moondog Show on WJW.

Jaworski said Mad Daddy's delivery on his commercials drew as much attention as his patter about the music and artists. He noted that delivery tells us a lot about the real Pete Myers. "With his delivery, and no notes, Mad Daddy had to be the real Pete Myers. He rhymed everything, even the commercials. I remember one night when some girl called in and requested a record. It was *Witch Doctor* and at the end of the request she said, 'Make something rhyme with witch doctor.' That's what he would do. You would call in a request, he'd play the song, and then he'd come back on and make something rhyme. We were riding around in the car, and we bet it was impossible. He could never do this. A minute and a half later, whatever it was, Myers comes back on and….I can't remember the exact words…but he said something about, 'The police was chasing him and that's how he clocked her. The witch doctor!"

While Myers as Mad Daddy relished the spotlight like any actor in front of an audience, his true love seemed to be his show. He was often introducing new elements, and on December 20, 1958 listeners heard a character named T. Smedley Rosewater, who was said to be a new member of the WHK staff. In reality, Myers would tape segments in a different voice while records were being played and play the tape back to have comical conversations with himself. It should also be pointed out that Myers did at least one appearance with someone standing in as Smedley and that was in a Sunday afternoon appearance at the Cleveland Arena in February 1959. The event was a championship 50 lap midget auto and motorcycle race with a special match race advertised between Mad Daddy and Smedley. There's no record of who might have taken on the role of Smedley. Myers sure knew how to work a crowd. He maintained his heavy schedule of personal appearances and was such a hit hosting the sock hops at the Garfield Armory in suburban Garfield Heights that he was offered the spot permanently as a sort of "residency".

Pete Myers' success as Mad Daddy in Cleveland drew the attention of WHK's sister station in New York City, WNEW. It offered Myers his big break into the New York market to replace Al "Jazzbo" Collins on the 8 to midnight shift, and Myers eagerly accepted. Cleveland fans were stunned! Jaworski said the news hit like a bombshell.

"I remember the last show. I remember the first announcement I heard, 'This is my last show.' We were in my buddy's mother's '57 mint green Plymouth four door sedan heading down Rocky River Drive, and he came on the radio to say, 'Doggone it. This is my very last show.' We were just devastated. We couldn't believe he made it to New York that fast. A lot of people like Alan Freed stepped up to New York. That wasn't uncommon. There was no need to listen to the radio anymore. I mean, what was there to listen to if he's gone? Half the show was the music, but the other half was him. Maybe the most important part of the show was him.

Pete Myers seemed to be at the top of his game and had become an icon to radio fans in Northeast Ohio.

Norm N. Nite observed it was simply a case of the right place at the right time.

"All the other guys on the air were just playing the records, had a nice delivery and everything else. But he created something related to teenagers. He came up with the phrases and was able to speak to the teenagers at that time on their level. He said things that they admired, and thought were cool, and they'd repeat them at school. I remember very, very vividly his last show. I remember his last song. LaVern Baker. *In the Dark*. When he said, 'The winky light is out' and everything else, all of us were just devastated. 'Pete Myers! He's leaving us!' He was only on the air for a short period of time at WHK and before that at WJW, but for the short period of time that he was here in Cleveland he made such an impact."

Pete Myers also had a new wife, Lisa, and a new challenge on a super-sized stage, New York City.

Chapter Five

"He Grows on You...Like a Fungus!"

New York was the dream of many broadcast professionals. It was the center of the industry in the biggest city in the country, and there was also talk that Myers would get a spot on WNEW-TV. Recalling his brother's career, Ernie Myers said he was "Delighted… and very proud of Pete's quick rise in radio." Just weeks before his New York debut, drunk with optimism about the new radio gig, Pete Myers announced he was planning to syndicate his "scream rock and roll show", tape it and send it out to stations across the country. There was hope that Mad Daddy would still have a presence in Northeast Ohio, though WHK would not commit to carrying the show when it was made available. In fact, they didn't even have a local replacement for Myers and stressed they were looking for "young talent"

There was a slight hitch that Myers did not anticipate. WNEW was not a top 40 rock station. It played what was known then as standards, and now as the Great American Songbook. The station hung its hat on artists like Frank Sinatra, Tony Bennett, Perry Como and similar artists. It was also the home of New York favorite William B. Williams, who made it clear to his audience that he hated rock and roll. Station management wanted Pete Myers as a straight announcer, but Myers successfully pleaded for a chance to do Mad Daddy on his opening night. WNEW agreed to allow Mad Daddy an on-air audition to test audience reaction.

Pete Myers debuted as the Mad Daddy on WNEW on Saturday, July 4, 1959, and did so with a great deal of pre-show publicity from the station. His Cleveland engineer Arnie Rosenberg would later say the move to New York was Myers' dream saying, "He wanted to be the biggest guy in the world." The dream lasted just one night.

The following Monday WNEW's phone lines were jammed from the moment the offices opened for business. In addition, more than 100 letters arrived and the response to Mad Daddy was not good. They included comments like "Who is that idiot?" and "What is he doing on WNEW?" Jack Sullivan met with Myers that same day, and published reports indicate both agreed Mad Daddy would not return to WNEW, though Myers was later said to be despondent over the move. Sullivan stressed to the New York newspapers that WNEW was not contemplating any format change, despite the rumors it might go Top 40, and promised Mad Daddy would never be heard again on his station. He said, "We're not going to copy any other station. We just want to make WNEW a better number one than ever." The TV offer was rescinded as well.

The trade press was brutal. At the time, *Billboard* magazine was the bible of the entertainment world, and it quoted Sullivan as saying he brought Myers in to replace Al "Jazzbo" Collins' spot on the roster because he sounded like a good fit for WNEW's "sophisticated" sound. Myers, that is, not Mad Daddy, though Sullivan was aware of his rock and roll roots. The article claimed Myers "pleaded for a chance" to introduce Mad Daddy to the New York audience, and Sullivan agreed to test the audience reaction. The magazine described the reaction as "vociferous", and it would be Mad Daddy's first and only appearance during Myers' during his initial run at the station.

New York was the biggest radio market in the world, and a far more cosmopolitan city than Cleveland. A great deal of the arts community and emerging counterculture was centered there. Mad Daddy would seem to be a sure hit in the Big Apple, but not at WNEW in 1959. However, as Myers' friend operatic tenor Ben Arrigo put it, "WNEW's format can't be tampered with. Big Broadway producers, politicians, and corporate executives listen to it. New York's stable upper-middle class. They got home and listened to this craziness? They were appalled."

It wasn't just the trades. Myers also had another thorn in his side and that was the *Beacon Journal's* radio-TV writer Dick Shippy. He plain didn't like rock and roll and it was painfully apparent that he really REALLY disliked Mad Daddy Myers. Shippy seemed to relish answering his critics in his column as well as potent and well-aimed digs at their hero. The events of July 1959 seemingly had him dancing on Daddy's grave. The headline in the *Akron Beacon Journal* pretty much said it all. It read, "Mad Daddy Muzzled", and Shippy loaded on Myers from there. He wrote, "When they get around to handing out certificates of merit for radio stations, I'll cast a ballot for station WNEW, New York City, which performed a distinct public service recently. It slapped a muzzle on disk jockey Pierre 'Pete' Myers, otherwise known as 'Mad Daddy'. (and in some regions as 'Mad Dog')." Got a feeling that was a tad bit of editorializing on Shippy's part.

More salt on the wound. "This is the same 'Mad Daddy' who assaulted ear drums as a deejay in Akron (WHKK) and Cleveland. It's the same 'Mad Daddy' who parachuted into Lake Erie where the Coast Guard fished him out for some reason unbeknownst to man." Just a thought. Maybe to save him from drowning?

"Myers promptly launched his New York career", wrote Shippy, "by antagonizing a good segment of his listening audience and by stirring up the station's top brass". Granted, this is pretty much accurate, but Shippy fails to mention WNEW's format which was not a first stop for rock and roll fans, though he does hint at it as the column continued.

In his review of Myer's debut, Shippy states, "Spinning records on an 8 p.m. to midnight show, Myers drew several hundred phone calls protesting his overwhelming indulgence in rock and roll music and insipid patter." (Ouch!) "By his third program, rock and roll had disappeared from Myers' show, replaced by the more sedate brand which is the station's trademark. Listeners also noted that Mad Daddy's personality had been subdued to the point where he was doing little more than announcing song titles. Which would be an obvious improvement." Now, this brings up an interesting point. There are no known recordings of Mad Daddy's New York debut. Did Shippy have some inside information that Myers continued the character after that first show, or was he simply referring to Myers' "lovable laughable" self?

More from the article. "A station spokesman said Myers was hired with the understanding that he would continue WNEW's regular policy on musical selections." While no documents have been produced to verify that, the station's immediate actions would seem to bear that out. "The spokesman added Myers was told to drop rock-and-roll 'not because of the telephone calls but because we didn't want this kind of thing in the first place'". Again, that seems likely, but Shippy fails to identify the source of the comments. A spokesman could be top management or the receptionist reading from a prepared statement. He finishes the piece by proclaiming, "Things is looking up, friends." How, and for who?

He didn't let up as the weeks continued, despite the fact that Myers was working hundreds of miles away. In one of his more polite responses (by Shippy standards) a reader unloaded both barrels at the writer stated, "Fathead, know nothing Shippy! If you had ever stopped to listen to Pete Myers, you might have found out what a good deejay is like. You may even get to like him! (Signed) MAD ABOUT MAD DADDY. Shippy responded, "Dear Mad. I understand he grows on you…like a fungus." A week later, Shippy went into greater detail about his distaste for "all things Mad Daddy" in a give and take with his young readers.

You could just picture a smiling Shippy rubbing his hands together in glee before pounding out his upcoming column. He used a letter written to him at the *Beacon Journal* as the cornerstone of his argument. It read, "Now that we know your views against Mad Daddy, I'm sure your teenage audience…what's left of it…would like to know your opinions of Dick Clark and some of our own Akron disc jockeys." It was followed by other reader barbs including, "You sound like the type that would try to keep babies from smiling because it causes wrinkles at 99", "Did you enjoy the black bottom or was yours the time of waltzes and minuets", and what seemed like an obvious point, "If New York hired him they knew or should have known what they were getting. In this modern age why not record it and push a button if all you want to hear is song titles." Let's think about this for a moment. Did WNEW have a Mad Daddy aircheck? Myers had early recording equipment and it's unlikely a station in the largest radio market in the U.S. would blindly hire an announcer based on a look at his ratings. It's a distinct possibility that Myers landed the job but convinced management to give Mad Daddy a shot. The readers continued the personal attacks on the writer. In a back handed slap one wrote, "You had better trade in your hick sense of humor for a pinch of young at heartedness. You had better pull down your old maid bonnet, your jealousy is showing. As for me, I'm a resigning fan of yours." It's important to note that in the 1950s, newspapers were still the main source of news for most, even younger readers. It wasn't until the immediacy of the Kennedy assassination in November 1963 that TV news started to surge, but until then newspapers and radio had the advantage. Now it was time for Shippy to respond and he came out swinging.

"Well, Mr. or Miss Resigning Fan. One of the objections I have to Pete Myers and his breed, and the music they shill for is that they have made a crusade out of playing rock-and-roll --- like defending freedom of speech." Don't song lyrics fall under the concept of speech? Shippy continued saying, "I don't believe a disc jockey should be compelled to conform to rock-and-roll." Then, as now, stations sell their formats. That format is developed by management and programmers and the disc jockey delivers the product. The hole in Shippy's argument is the same concept that had him doing back flips for Myers New York failure in New York. Myers didn't follow format.

There's more. "I don't believe all listeners should have to conform to rock-and-roll. And as things stand now, too often it's a case of either you like it or lump it. And radio then moves backward." Okay, this is proven wrong on a number of levels. Right next to Shippy's article on that very same page are the radio schedules and on Akron's main stations (WAKR, WASC, WCUE and WHKK) you could see a wide variety of programming including religion, news, drama, comedies and music. There were also plenty of Cleveland outlets booming into the Rubber City with a wide range of shows and personalities. Years later, in 2012, the Beach Boys' Brian Wilson wrote, "That's Why God Made the Radio". He also created the radio dial and the on / off switch. If the station wasn't playing the format Shippy wanted at the time he wanted, he could have contacted the station's management, turned the dial or tried that television thing that was becoming more popular in homes across the region. In the case of Pete Myers, Shippy was targeting the messenger more so than the message.

"There's just no middle ground", he claimed, "for those of us who like the comparative peace of Dave Brubeck, or Ella Fitzgerald." Not buying it. There were plenty of opportunities to hear them and other artists. "And for somebody who digs chamber music, they're stuck so far out on a limb it's a three-day bus ride back." We'll just leave that one there for you to consider.

Shippy continued. "How about a little peaceful coexistence? If the musical world could work out something along those lines, it might encourage the efforts of capitalism and Communism." Again, whatever that is supposed to mean is probably best interpreted by the reader, but Shippy does admit that he does not believe rock-and-roll to be a legitimate emerging art form. "Actually, a person is in error in consenting to argue the pros and cons of rock and roll. You wind up attaching a greater significance to this form than it deserves, losing sight that there are more important matters in the universe.". Question: Then why is Mr. Shippy arguing the pros and cons?

In response to the question about his musical tastes, Shippy stressed, "Mine was and is the time of Artie Shaw, Glenn Miller, Woodie Herman, Tommy Dorsey, Charlie Barnett..." and a paragraph more of classic jazz names. He states ominously, "If this is the graveyard of music, then let me rest in peace. But Fabian and 'The Tiger'? Not if I can help it." This was a reference to Fabian's 1959 hit song. Finally, Shippy adds, "And, all this wild, lunatic fringe chatter? Friends, Dizzy Gillespie was talking like that years ago, but he could complement it with talent." After a few cracks about marketing products to youth he finishes with, "Enough is enough, I say." At first glance it would seem Shippy is okay with the lingo he protested as long as it came from his favorite jazz artists.

In fact, his attacks on Mad Daddy continued for years after. He was still on Shippy's mind in 1960 when he wrote, "Pete 'Mad Daddy' Myers, who used to assault Akron eardrums before moving on Cleveland station WHK and then to New York City, now is a fine music deejay at WNEW in New York. *Radio-TV Daily* promotes him as a graduate of London University and the Royal Academy of Dramatic Arts. If so, he managed to hide it during his Akron hitch." Shippy's obsession with Myers surfaced again in 1963 when asked by a *Beacon Journal* reader if WJW-TV's major star "Ghoulardi" played by Ernie Anderson (who worked with Myers at WHK) had also played "Mad Daddy". If not, the reader asked for clarification and Shippy shot back, "'Mad Daddy is a je---, I mean a jentleman (sic) named Pete Myers and the last I heard he was chipping away at the sanity of New Yorkers." It didn't stop there. A final, if somewhat softer dig was lobbed at Myers in a front-page question in the *Beacon Journal's* "Action Line", a popular column that claimed it "solves problems, cuts red tape, gets answers, investigates your complaints and stands up for your rights". You'd call in your concern to a phone number listed under the logo and in December 1966, a former Kent State University student from Rocky River outside Cleveland asked, "What ever happened to Mad Daddy?" Shippy's by-line is nowhere to be found but it certainly carried on his negative spirit against Myers. The answer read, "Mad Daddy has given up the cape bit, the far out poetry that went from bad to verse. He's now just plain Pete Myers from 1 to 4 p.m. weekdays on WNEW in New York. He tried the Mad Daddy routine briefly and all it got him was a Bronx cheer. WNEW has sent a picture (which was included in the column) of your hero. He hardly seems mad at all anymore." To be fair to Shippy and his fans, he was hired to offer his opinion on local media and while it may seem overtly biased and at times misguided, he was doing the job he was hired to do. Let's get back to New York 1959.

Norm N. Nite claimed Mad Daddy's quick failure would lead to bouts of depression for Myers. "He had hoped things were going to take off like in Cleveland, and when it didn't it had to bother him. When you have an ego in radio like that, you succeed in one market… Like Alan Freed. He was here (in Cleveland) and he became bigger in New York. Here's a situation where you had a highly talented guy (Myers) yet it just didn't work."

Ernie Myers also said that he noticed his brother falling into depression. Few people back in the late fifties and early sixties owned home recording equipment. It was expensive and bulky, and few saw any need to own that type of gear. There were some hi-fi enthusiasts who invested in tape machines, but most used them for music reproduction. As a result, there is precious little audio footage of Pete Myers. However, some audio does exist, and in a recording from Myers' July 26, 1961, show on WNEW we hear a far more sedate announcer introducing songs like Helen O'Connell's "All of Me" and Dave Brubeck's "Take Five". He also made an impression on the young audience in New York.

Sirius radio programmer Walt Sabo says, "Well, I've spent my life in radio in New York and when I was in high school he did 1-4 on WNEW. I am a New York Pete Myers fan." He also recalled, "On WNEW as urbane, soft spoken Pete, he would occasionally ID himself as, 'I'm Pete Myers..(long pause)… The Mad Daddy on WNEW." But Sabo was in for a surprise regarding Myers saying, "I knew Pete only as the one on WNEW. I was head of programming at Sirius and one of the jocks mentioned to me about Pete's technical tricks as the Mad Daddy. And I had no idea. Then I listened to the airchecks. I took (Myers' producer) Neil McIntyre to lunch to learn more." At the time, Myers seemed perfectly at home in that format, though his fans still held fond memories of Mad Daddy.

In the days before the British Invasion of the mid-Sixties and following the surge of rock and roll's first wave idled, in part, by the payola scandals, programmers played it safe which could also be interpreted as boring. The search was on for something new to bring in the audience while avoiding controversy. By spring 1960, Bruce Morrow was now including a *Folk Song 15* segment along with the Top 40 of the day. Later on, it was older tunes in the *Musical Museum,* while other programmers in New York and across the country experimented with everything from comedy cuts to Broadway show tunes. Some flat out banned rock and roll, with one Texas station premiering a format it called "Refined Radio" that screamed easy listening with little to attract a young audience with expendable cash. Even the innovators were limited in what they could offer. In Cleveland, the legendary Bill Randle at WERE…. named one of the top trend spotters in the U.S ... was experimenting with light jazz, and Myers and Bill Williams at WNEW did the same, offering Oscar Peterson, George Shearing and the like. One can only wonder what Myers was thinking when comparing his current show to the Mad Daddy in Cleveland, but he had steady employment and still held out hope that his alter ego could be revived.

Elvis Presley's hitch in the Army was drawing to an end in 1960, leaving active duty on March 5th. It wasn't like he was going to have to look for work on his return because the radio audience was eager to have him back, and radio stations worked overtime to exploit the promotional possibilities. Presley's film *Jailhouse Rock* (1957) was rushed back to 200 theaters nationwide, and in New York WNEW gearing up for his return to civilian life. Here's the issue: WNEW's format wasn't the same type of raucous rock and roll that broke Presley nationwide, the station's William B. Williams made it clear that wasn't his type of music and Pete Myers was on a leash as far as the format was concerned. Still, you couldn't ignore the promotional value of an event every other station was poised to jump on as soon as Presley landed, so WNEW issued a statement assuring its audience that "We will sprinkle Presley samples through the program on this basis: Enough to illustrate the major points made and to satisfy Presley worshippers, but not so much as to alienate anyone who thinks he should have signed up for another hitch in the Army". As promised, WNEW had heavy coverage of his return in its hourly newscasts along with numerous spins of a Presley song more attuned with their audience, "Love Me Tender". In a way it was reflective of the way they treated Myers and his abilities.

Rock and roll radio has traditionally focused its attention on a young audience and in 1960 that meant after school hours were prime time. Longtime WNEW voice Lonny Starr let the station that April resulting in new assignments for the remaining staff and Pete Myers was changed to 8 to 10 p.m. The later hours gave him some freedom with a seemingly built-in audience looking for the latest hits, even though the playlists of the day could seem somewhat saccharin. It was still Myers' job and he worked with what he was given.

Whether he was prompted by the station or simply wanting to keep peace with WNEW, Myers was asked by *Billboard* magazine what three albums he would want if he was stranded on a desert island with a portable phonograph. He wrote, "Funny you should ask. Although you are referring to pop albums, my three-volume library would include the new Columbia Symphony version of "Le Sacre du Printemps" with the composer conducting; the Decca London Symphony's Scheherazade and the Warner Bros edition of Gershwin's "Rhapsody in Blue".

He went on to say, "If it must be a list of my 'druthers' in the pop category, the I would include Frank Sinatra's "Come Fly with Me", Victor's "Glenn Miller Yesterday" album, and any old Julie London album." You can also bet he wrote with a smile on his face, "Leave the record home – all I want is the cover portrait for spiritual and intellectual upliftment." Noticeably absent were "Greasy Chicken" and other songs that laid the foundation for his journey to New York radio.

He certainly kept himself busy in and out of the studio. Pete Myers still pursued acting gigs, and while at WNEW got theater jobs as well as roles on TV's *Hallmark Hall of Fame (1959)*. In addition, Myers was named spokesman for Pepperidge Farm Cookies, which sponsored his show on WNEW.

It should also be noted that Myers still enjoyed a wide range of interests, and most were unrelated. He had a love for Eastern culture from his days in the military, a respect for firearms, and a passion for the speed and energy of sports cars. So, when Myers was given the opportunity to comment on WNEW about the latest roadsters he jumped at the chance. The station featured his *Sports Car Extra* vignettes on weekends starting that August, which also Myers an inside route to test drive the new models before they made it to the showroom. People loved cars…but they hated traffic! Myers saw an opportunity to capitalize on the frustration of New York commuters. It didn't take long for rookie drivers to have horror stories, and Myers wanted to hear them in his "Bumper to Bumper" contest asking listeners to share their most hair-raising experiences coming in or out of Manhattan. The payoff? Five winners were chosen and were chauffeured to their jobs for a week in Rolls Royces.

Drive-time then, as now, is a crucial part of the radio day. Radio stations were always looking for something the audience could relate too, and had a captive audience in rush hour, especially in the long trek in and out of New York City. It only seemed natural that a stunt or promotion connected to the journey to and from the job would draw an audience, and the New York rush hour was particularly challenging. Stations across the country tried variations of exploiting the long ride home to freedom, but WNEW had a *Crosstown Test* to determine just how difficult that daily ride was. It centered on the epicenter of frustration, midtown Manhattan, with a tongue in cheek look at what might be the fastest and most efficient form of travel.

Each of the WNEW jocks was issued a different type of transportation in a race to see who could move about the fastest. They were also assigned a chorus girl from the Broadway show *Do Re Mi* for the ride. Folks lined the streets to cheer on their favorites with Bob Landers at the station doing race commentary with remote reports from Hans Anderson and Ike Pappas. The route was East 51ˢᵗ Street from the East River to the Hudson and clearly, some of the participants had a distinct edge. When the flag went down at the finish line it was Gene Klavan racing across on a Vespa bike with a time of 16 minutes 30 seconds. Behind by just ten seconds to take second place was Dee Finch in a cab, William B. Williams rolled up in a Rolls Royce to take third at 19 minutes 45 seconds (like he was in a hurry riding in the luxury of a Rolls). Pete Myers was in a horse and carriage that took 24 minutes and 15 seconds to finish with Kyle Rote bringing up the rear at 28 minutes 45 seconds. Keep in mind this was crossing midtown. Good for a laugh, but the long ride then as now often goes more than an hour if you're lucky and the wind is at your back.

There's a long-held theory that much of 1960s pop culture was taken over by the "Three B's", that being James Bond films, Batman on TV and the Beatles. That may be an oversimplification, but it points to the media's focus on the growing influence of youth and expendable cash. A good example of that might be *The Ed Sullivan Show* (1948) which offered a wide variety of acts weekly in a type of televised vaudeville, with the savvy Sullivan also recognizing the need to appeal to younger audiences primarily with musical acts. Shows like the *Hollywood Palace* (1964) and *This is Tom Jones* (1969), among others, would follow similar formats. Myers had a good understanding of the still developing social and economic power of the boomer generation and combined it effectively with Mad Daddy's mix of *Famous Monsters of Filmland* and EC Comics imagery, *Mad* magazine humor and, of course, rhythm and blues. But he wasn't a TV personality. He became frustrated with the medium in Cleveland, though he did try acting a few times on stage and the small screen with varying degrees of success and notoriety. His medium of choice was the theater of the mind, and he used audio like a painter's palette with sound effects as his color.

AM radio at the time was also discovering long playing albums, and it wasn't to go off their music play lists. Their FM counterparts had been using spoken word recordings to fill time, but some of the hottest up and coming comedians were putting out LPs and toured to promote them. Shelley Berman, Mort Sahl, Bob Newhart and others found new fans that might never enter a night club, and AM programmers were keen to air album cuts and even get the comics in the studio. Granted, some of the material was pretty racy. "Moms" Mabley, Redd Foxx, Rusty Warren had some fall down funny material with their party records but they "worked blue" and the person at the mic had better know when to cut the track before something that didn't belong on the air got out. Programmers urged the record labels to tone it down or put out disc jockey promo copies suitable for airplay. There was also a good reason for the rise of comedy LP other than the vanilla sound of most records of the time. The world was a dangerous place. The fight for civil rights in a racially polarized America, the Cold War prior to the upcoming Cuban Missile Crisis, growing campus unrest and any number of other concerns had people looking for something to escape to. Pete Myers saw that need and used it to his advantage on his WNEW show..

Myers was getting plenty of attention in a comfortable job in the world's largest radio market. He was respected by his radio peers and had a sizable audience, and other industry folks liked him as well. Bill Gavin was a highly regarded free-lance record programmer who conducted an annual poll of the radio and record people who made the most significant and contributions to the radio industry and in 1962 he named Myers along with other heavy hitters such as Dick Biondi at Chicago's WLS, and KMPC's Julie Rizzo to the list,. Another significant name he singled out was a familiar one. It was Neil McIntyre at Cleveland's WHK, who would continue to play a significant role in Myer's career.

In 1962, seemingly content to be working New York radio, Myers decided to branch out once again and give novelty records another shot. Another former Clevelander now on staff at WNEW was former disc jockey Phil McLean, now doing news, and he was getting attention for his "Small Sad Sam", on the Versatile label responding to Jimmy Dean's "Big Bad John". What was odd about McLean's record was that it was issued under his name. WNEW management wasn't happy about that move "because of the public's general mage of the dignity of a newsman". McLean followed that up with another song, "Big Mouth Bill", which some saw as a slam against his former co-worker at WERE, the legendary Bill Randle.

William B. Williams had a spoken word Christmas LP released and other jocks around town were having success with their albums including Murray Kaufman at WINS with his *Murray the K's Sing Along with the Original Golden Gassers,* as well as *Murray the K's Blasts from the Past*, and Alan Freed made it to the charts with his *Memory Lane* album. Across the river in New Jersey WNTA's Clay Cole and WNJR's George Hudson were on turntables and Myers decided the time was right for his return to the recording studio.

The result was a 45 titled "Gunga Didn't" backed with "Morse Code" on Mr. Peacock Records. Both tunes are credited to songwriter A. Boyce, but Myers is billed as Lord Didd, and is backed up on the flip side by a group called "the Didn'ts", likely his take on Dickey Do and the Don'ts who charted with "Ballad of a Train" a few years before. This begs the question why Myers would use a pseudonym while Williams and McLean used their given names? As with most recordings of the type, it had a short shelf life and Myers wasn't through yet.

Recognizing the safe but bland recordings on his station's playlists, and the need for additional programming elements, comedy records seemed a logical choice and Myers was well equipped to capitalize on their popularity especially after the response to "Gunga Didn't". The top songs of that year included Shelley Fabares "Johnny Angel", "Stranger on the Shore" by Mr. Acker Bilk, and "Roses are Red (My Love)" from Bobby Vinton among others that might produce a slight smile before a yawn. Novelty songs that year were getting lots of attention, including Bobby (Boris) Pickett's "Monster Mash", "My Boomerang Won't Come Back" by Charlie Drake,

TV's "Beaver" Jerry Mathers with "Don' Cha Cry" and dozens of others. Not all were based on humor. The guy who played Grandpappy Amos McCoy, Walter Brennan, sang about a beloved mule with "Old Rivers", the Shenandoah Three paid tribute to a film star with "The Ballad of Marilyn Monroe", and the racy album *Sexarama* by Miss Dee with a cover that couldn't be displayed. Even so, continuing a creative streak that began in Cleveland with the Joker's "I Love a Practical Joke / What is a Fisteris?", Myers wrote "Operations Decoy" about recent reports that New York policemen were dressing as women to lure and catch muggers. It was released on Laurie Records under the name Hugh Masher that some speculated was Myers himself at the mic. The single got a favorable review in *Billboard* stating it could "develop easily as a comedy smash" and, while not suggesting Myers might be the voice, adding "the singer gives it lot of punch and his comedy timing is good.".

Myers also had a side business offering humorous content to radio stations. The so-called "continuity drop in bits" ran from 60 to 90 seconds from a service he called "Dinky Dramas, Inc.", which got a plug from free-lance programmer Bill Gavin in *Billboard*... but there was something else in that issue that may have been a premonition of things to come for Myers' career. WINS had a format described as similar to WNEW's, and a headline story in that same issue read, "Sale of WINS Might Mean a Return to Rock". Could it also eventually mean a return of the Mad Daddy?

There were connections to Cleveland where Myers was still considered a legend. Sports announcer Bob Neal, half of the WJW Indians play by play team, visited New York with the team in July 1962 and hosted a post-game show on WERE radio from the lobby of the Biltmore Hotel. Along with Indians players and management Neal welcomed former WTAM-AM announcer Johnny Andrews and as well as Myers who stopped by to share memories.

If Myers could draw any comfort from the uncertainty over his position at WNEW, what he wanted to do and where he was heading, it came from an unlikely source. His wife, Ann, said along with her there was another fan who pledged undying loyalty and that was their Siamese cat, who usually had an aversion to radio. However, when Myers voice would come on during his shift the cat would race over and park himself on top of the radio "purring happily through the commercials". Just a few years before hobbyists were listening to crude "cat's whisker" radio sets! The tables had turned!

Myers spent four years at WNEW building a loyal and solid audience, but in 1963 a fateful reunion would open new doors for Myers and his alter ego. An offer came from New York's top-rated rock station WINS, which was also home to the highly popular disc jockey "Murray the K" Kaufmann. The offer came from program director Neil McIntyre, the same Neil McIntyre who worked as an intern for Myers' Cleveland stations and later acted as his assistant. McIntyre sold WINS management on the idea that Myers…and possibly Mad Daddy …were the kind of unique entertainers that New York was looking for.

Chapter Six

Sponge Rubber Heaven

Westinghouse Broadcasting signed Myers to WINS at the same time it brought on former WIL / St. Louis jock Dick Clayton in a move that many saw as a much needed "face lift" for the Top 40 outlet. GM Mark Olds told Billboard the two new additions to the staff was meant to combine "the best of the new talent from local and out-of-town sources with the successful performers already at hand" though failing to mention the so-called "new talent' could also be seen as seasoned pros. More known names were also being courted to play in the WINS sandbox.

Pete Myers accepted the job and Mad Daddy took the airwaves at 1010 WINS. The *Daily News'* Charles McHarry wrote in his column in July 1963 about, "Manhattan's newest disc jockey? He calls himself Mad Daddy and he dresses like a ghoul. His patter is from Nutsville but he spins a lot of hits. He's heard over WINS from 11 PM to midnight on Saturdays." There was even a photo of Myers in his cowl as Daddy, but reactions were mixed. Was he too hip for New York? What about the time slot? It's hard to pin down why Mad Daddy didn't hit at the time. John Zacherley had been doing a similar horror host character on TV since 1958 in Philadelphia and New York as host of the *Shock Theater* Universal Studios film package and had a hit with a novelty record called *Dinner with Drac*. Ernie Anderson's "Ghoulardi", which was based in good part on his time watching Myers' Mad Daddy at WHK, skyrocketed to fame in Cleveland on WJW-TV's *Shock Theater*. TV may have been the key because Myers continued to do Mad Daddy exclusively on radio.

Myers' decision to move on to WINS begins what Jay Hunt said is the third and final major phase of the Mad Daddy character. He noted that, "Myers retained his old persona, but it was greatly toned down and the show was just a shadow of its WHK days. The playlist would eventually include typical top forty hits of the period, Neil Sedaka, Bobby Darren, The Supremes, even Peter, Paul and Mary. (He must have hated that!) Advertising was a mixed bag appealing to a multi-demographic, newspapers, gum, beer, Broadway performances etc. He still did dedications but even they were greatly toned down and he frequently begged for cards and letters to keep his show on the air.

Keeping in mind that Meyers' tenure at WINS was during the Kennedy Administration, the fabled "Age of Camelot", he was keen to play cuts from a comedy album that was breaking sales records and that was Vaughn Meader and Friends' *The First Family*. The demand for the LP was overwhelming and pressing plants worked around the clock to have enough product for the Christmas season. At the time, Meader was an unknown comic but his label, Cadence Records, had enough faith in him to think the LP would sell as many as 100,000 copies. It did. Within days of being released a copy found its way to Stan Burns at WINS who saw its value and kept playing tracks during his show to a wild response. Myers knew a good thing when he heard it and he put it in heavy rotation during his shift that same day. WHN's Bob and Ray liked what they heard, as did the jocks at Myers' old stomping ground WNEW, and it wasn't long before just about every station in New York was airing cuts firing demand for the album. Record stores couldn't keep up with requests. There just wasn't enough product and radio wasn't about to stop playing the endless stream of requests for Meader and company. Pressing plants in Indianapolis and Los Angeles worked around the clock, though printing the four-color cover was also a challenge. Within weeks of its release the LP was now being produced at ten plants nationwide with four printing plants pressing covers. The response was stunning, the album was a smash hit and it showed the power of radio in appealing to an audience hungry for something new. Myers' style of radio seemed to make a lot more sense. He was now under pressure to show he could draw an audience without Vaughn Meader and was still confident Mad Daddy was the key.

Pete Myers felt a bit more freedom at WINS. It was a younger audience, a more contemporary format and while it didn't have the audience WNEW boasted he still saw brighter days ahead. It also meant he could develop his own brand of humor often based on the headlines. While it didn't match his Godzilla in Tokyo Bay from years before, Myers did raise some eyebrows with a campaign to locate 919 acres of swamp land in New Jersey so the state could qualify its Great Jersey swamp as a Federal Game Preserve. He asked listeners for suggestions and the letters started pouring in. One suggested the Fordham University parking lot, another the entire community of Far Rockaway and more than a few that didn't get used on the air.

There's another odd twist noted by Walt Sabo who recalls, "He was the official station voice, doing the legal ID on WINS sounding sartorial. Those announcements would play during the Mad Daddy show and all day, and you would never guess it was the same person." Myers had done a great job separating his alter ego from "lovable laughable Pete".

He certainly knew how to generate publicity. Citing what the *Daily News* called his "far out show", Daddy got press during Britain's Profumo scandal, when Prime Minister Harold Macmillan's Secretary of State for War admitted sharing a relationship with 19-year old call girl Christine Keeler who was also seeing a Soviet naval attaché. Daddy took to the air suggesting the hottest items in Paris were British postcards. (Topical humor that obviously faded with time.) Plus, Mad Daddy tapped into New York's love of baseball announcing he'd formed a group with some home team fans called "Mets Anonymous". The 1963 season was only the second for the still new Mets and their record was dismal at best. Daddy's idea was to grab any member who was thinking about rooting for a winning team and have another member drive him around in an Edsel until the urge left them.

Myers even tried syndicating Mad Daddy for a brief time, broadcasting nightly from the imaginary Sponge Rubber Heaven to stations like WPOP / Hartford. Ernie Myers recalled visiting his brother in New York and sitting in to observe one of the syndicated shows, and said he seemed happier, but tired. He still played Mad Daddy to the hilt, but the style of radio and music that helped sell the character was passing by rapidly. The early sixties saw the emergence of Motown, surf music and the Philadelphia R & B sound, and radio formatting was becoming tighter and more controlled. It certainly wasn't the style of entertainment that took him to the top in Cleveland some years back, but it was play by the new rules or don't play at all.

Myers also took note of new trends in recording equipment that were expensive even for radio stations but starting to show up among home stereo hobbyists. He pored over recordings as he continued to develop and refine his on-air work as Daddy not only rehearsing new bits at home but also reviewing what worked in past shows that might also reach out not only to his current fans but an audience that was yet to discover him.

The Pete Myers side of his personae did quite well at WINS and was profiled in a 1963 *Billboard* piece looking at what he played and what he felt was the appeal of his show. Keeping in mind this was pre-British Invasion, a look at the playlist reflects a trend toward safe music with an emphasis on middle of the road programming. Henry Mancini's "Moon River", "It's Up to You" by Rick Nelson, the Rooftop Singers' "Walk Right In", and Kenny Ball's "Midnight in Moscow" all shared the airwaves with new releases from Frank Ifield and Jaye P. Morgan, with an occasional novelty tune like Allan Sherman's "Won't You Come Home Disraeli" and Ray Stevens' "Ahab the Arab". The only tune that might even draw a second look if only for its title was "The Stripper" by David Rose, and that was left up to the listener's imaginations. Myers is quoted as saying, "variety is the keynote of his programming policy" while at the same time noting his time at the mic was limited because of a heavy commercial load (which was music to the ears of management) and additional newscasts thanks to the New York newspaper strike. Even so, Myers had a good amount of control over his music and he tried to use only a minimal amount of past hits in favor of newer releases, stating his "extra material is used for pacing and color."

By 1964, the music world was in for an earth-shaking transition. Following the long mourning period from the assassination of John Kennedy on November 22, 1963 and a brutal winter over the northern United States, much of the country was ready for some hint of optimism and that came from England in February 1964. The Beatles debuted on the Ed Sullivan show on February 9, beginning the so-called "British Invasion" of European pop bands. Having lived and studied in London ten years before, Myers immediately saw the appeal and potential of the Beatles and drew side glances from his colleagues at WINS when he said the act would be bigger than Elvis Presley. In fact, Myers made it his business to be at LaGuardia Airport when the group landed to cheering crowds, handing out Beatle wigs and promotional t-shirts. The start of this second British Invasion sparked a drastic change in music and marketing to the youth culture, but sadly, a passing of the era that Myers embraced as the Mad Daddy.

Myers hadn't lost hope entirely that his and Mad Daddy's star could rise even further than his current situation at WINS. The British Invasion had brought a new energy to radio and entertainment, WPIX-TV had the "Cool Ghoul" John Zacherle hosting everything from *Chiller Theater* to cartoon shows, and his old WHK newsman Ernie Anderson was a TV superstar in Cleveland playing Ghoulardi which had a passing resemblance to Daddy. In the fall of 1964, Myers signed a long-term contract with the Ashley-Steiner-Famous Artists talent agency. Myers had an impressive resume, but whether the agency could market his particular brand of mayhem was anyone's guess….and time was running out at WINS.

Personality radio was still a vital component of the media, but it evolved with music. Change was also in the wind at WINS in early '64 as Myers' former coworker at WHK / Cleveland, Johnny Holliday, was announced as his replacement on the 10 p.m. to 2 a.m. slot starting February 17th. Myers was reassigned to a less desirable position earlier in the evening following Murray the K's *Swinging Soiree*, though he would also have a two-hour Daddy Saturday night show 'til midnight. Sadly, it didn't last long. On December 2nd, it was announced that Mad Daddy's last show on the station would be that Friday, just two days later. He was replaced by a 90-minute talk show, *Contact*, hosted by Stan Bernard that had previously been heard at midnight with Murray Burnett after the Mad Daddy show. It was an omen of things to come for the audience. In less than a year, on April 18, 1965, WINS would go to an all-news format. It may have been doomed to failure. Walt Sabo points out, "WINS was not a big stage. It was the third entry top-40 after WABC and WMCA which made any success on WINS for any one very hard." The management finally threw in the towel.

Chapter Seven

A Bigger Stage

Late February 1965 saw Pete Myers leave WINS to return to WNEW, the highly rated middle-of-the-road outlet airing songs by artists such as Frank Sinatra and Barbra Streisand, but it also provided a secure position in the world's largest media market. He replaced Wally King on the night-time schedule, and King was moved to fill the spot left by Fred Robbins who was shown the door. It was the same station where he briefly premiered Mad Daddy, though it was stressed in the press that he would not revive the character this time around. Myers was back to being a mellow voiced disc jockey providing patter between records, and while he did have some degree of job security, at 40 years old he was not confident about his future. But consider this. Walt Sabo tells us WNEW was not a bad place to be, saying "Interestingly all of the pieces on him refer to his failure to make the Mad Daddy work. What they don't mention is that doing 1-4 PM on WNEW was a much greater radio success!!! He was paid top dollar at the biggest and most influential adult music station in America. Every jock in America wanted to work there. Many auditioned, huge guys, and they would melt during the audition because it was such a big freakin' deal---when he was on the station it was wayyyyy # 1 Adults 25-54, minted money. The fact that they hired him back is a testament to his talent and professionalism---they could have hired any on air talent in America. Anyone!"

Myers' exit to WNEW was announced at a time when management in New York still wasn't sure where to put him. The station's Jack Sullivan still hadn't decided on a time slot when Myers made his departure from Cleveland known, but he was sure he had a winner. At the time, WNEW was owned by Metropolitan Broadcasting Corporation which had taken over WHK and its sister station a few months before and Myers was the only jock asked to stay on. Sullivan had obviously heard of the Mad Daddy character, but couldn't have foreseen his effect on the Gotham audience.

The expected WINS format change might have seemed odd at the time as advertisers looked for "young money" and the British Invasion led by "Beatlemania" was at its peak. "Murray the K" Kaufman was also at his peak, and he wasn't prepared to go quietly. WINS had been toning down the "screamers", the high energy jocks that drove the programming". Kaufman learned about the upcoming format switch, broke the news about the change without the station's or Group W's approval and resigned on the air effective February 27.

Myers' limited syndication continued, and there was talk of a British Mad Daddy TV show catering to the British Invasion crowd but it never got beyond the talking stages. Myers seemed enthusiastic about the British offer, because it would have given him an opportunity to educate and entertain at the same time. As he told WZAK's Dick Liberatore in 1967, it would have provided him a chance to reintroduce Mad Daddy to a new audience. "It was a lot of fun. Sure, I would. As a matter of fact there was a period when a couple of people in England were interested in putting it on the air in a Carnaby Street bit over there, when they discovered rock and roll. Actually, all the Beatle records and the Rolling Stones are 'steals' from old American rhythm and blues songs. These kids in London and up in Liverpool bought a lot of these old records that were part and parcel of the American scene. That was a whole new bag in England. The groups they bounced back from us kind of ricocheted in England."

He went on to praise Big Bill Broonzy, Howling Wolf, Lightnin' Slim and Screamin' Jay Hawkins. "They're rediscovered in England. They're a brand-new bag there. They're part and parcel of a traditional form of American music, rhythm and blues, which it is and they hadn't heard this prior to about 1955."

Myers was in a position that most disc jockeys would have loved to be in. He had a steady job in the world's largest media market and was pursuing a number of additional opportunities. But Myers saw it in a different way. He was consumed by ambition and rationalized his position as a small fish in a big pond of 10-million listeners.

It also should be considered that Myers may have been stuck in a phase of broadcasting that had passed by both him and the industry. The day when a disc jockey chose his own songs changed rapidly after the payola scandals of the fifties. The industry now anointed the program director with the final say on what acts got airtime. Play lists now pretty much ruled the industry, with an emphasis on major label acts with the promotional muscle to make stars. Plus, the emphasis also was placed on playing more music, with less between record patter from the disc jockeys. Another factor was that record companies could direct "promotional" money to certain program directors to use as they liked. Individuality was fading from radio stations across the country.

It is also vital to closely examine Cleveland's importance as a breakout market for radio talent. In the 1950s, Cleveland radio presented major air personalities like Bill Randle, Tommy Edwards, Bill Gordon and Alan Freed. As Jay Hunt observed, "Mad Daddy was a perfect follow-up to pioneer Alan Freed in Cleveland. That was a key to his success there. Why he failed in New York is a bit of a mystery. Perhaps it was because he was such a radical departure from anything WNEW had done before that their audience just couldn't accept him. Later on at WINS he again became popular, even with a try at syndicating his show, but he was never the same, being severely limited in his choice of music by the strict top 40 format and the Drake formula."

(Note: Drake was a highly structured format developed by the late Bill Drake that stressed less disc jockey patter, fewer commercials and more music presented in a tight schedule of presentation.)

Greg Miller said the New York programmers may not have understood Myers' act or the audience he appealed to. Miller added, "He may have not been marketed correctly in New York. I don't know that he was on the right station. They weren't ready for him. Another thing that is lesser known is that he was also one of the first late night TV movie hosts. In the late 1950s you had these late-night movie hosts, and Pete Myers made that transition. It was a double feature on Friday nights, and he had the same schtick…the cape and the pancake makeup, and he hosted the movie. That never took off, but when you look at the phenomena that started here in Cleveland with Ernie Anderson and Ghoulardi, and so on, it's a genre that always seemed to find a home here in Cleveland."

Miller says Cleveland TV, as in the case of New York's radio programmers, may not have been ready at the time to exploit Mad Daddy's true appeal. Ernie Anderson's Ghoulardi was a local television phenomenon due in great part to Anderson marketing the character himself through personal appearances.

Cleveland's reputation as a breakout market for music and personalities may have been at its peak at that time. Jay Hunt suggested, "Cleveland in the 1950s was where the innovations in pop radio in the Northeast happened. Alan Freed, Bill Randle, and Pete Myers all picked up southern R&B, rockabilly and rock and roll and brought it to northern listeners before anyone else did. They exported the concept to Chicago, Buffalo, Detroit and New York. The Cleveland audience was ripe for new things and Mad Daddy was the coolest thing on the air in 1958. New York was a different scene. They already had established patterns, Harlem blues, bebop, jazz and Tin Pan Alley pop and didn't crave something new the way we did."

It's also a possibility that the New York audience was more sophisticated and found Mad Daddy too extreme. Perhaps if he had gone to a different radio station whose main audience were teens looking for something new, he would have had a far different impact. Hunt suggested if public or alternative radio had existed back then he would have found an ideal home, though even today that type of radio draws a very small and select audience and is not especially lucrative for the programmers or air talent. Myers wanted a bigger stage.

Norm N. Nite isn't so sure and said you can't take your radio audience with you from market to market. He observed, "Certain things happen in certain places and certain markets, but for some reason or another it didn't fly in New York. It depressed him because he was so big here in Cleveland at what he was doing when he was on the air. It wasn't catching on. People didn't go for it. It bothered him, and then he had to change his style and he became just 'laughable, lovable Pete Myers' on WNEW. That's what got to him, when they changed his shift. They wanted to put him on in evenings after being on all those years in the afternoon. He just couldn't take it. He was such a talented artist, and when things didn't work the way he wanted it affected him greatly."

Anger gets you nothing but a reputation in just about any business. There's an old saying in radio not to burn bridges because you'll work with a lot of people more than once at different stations and this was a prime example. Myers was originally recruited for WNEW by its PD Mark Olds who heard him on WHK while doing the same job at KYW in Cleveland. Oddly enough, WNEW's general manager Harvey Glascock held a similar position at WHK when Myers was there so it shows the best way to say goodbye was a handshake. They also knew Myers capabilities which may have assured him continued employment, though it was also evident that he was starting to change.

In 1966, Myers received a visit from two Cleveland friends, WJW-TV's Ernie "Ghoulardi" Anderson and Tim Conway, the Chagrin Falls, Ohio, native who played Ensign Charles Parker on ABC-TV's *McHale's Navy* (1962). They had worked together at Cleveland TV stations in the past and were promoting their comedy album on Liberty Records titled, *Bull!* However, despite using comedy cuts in the past, Myers couldn't promote the record because the program director didn't feel its content fit the format. While disappointed, the two understood the situation Myers found himself in and used the opportunity to renew old acquaintances. However, Anderson, Neil McIntyre and Arnie Rosenberg, who stayed in touch with Myers, also noticed a gradual personality change in both his voice and demeanor.

Chapter Eight

"Are you Happy You're Back in Cleveland?"

Personal problems had apparently affected Myers. He divorced his wife Ann, the dancer from Ohio, and remarried a New York model named Lisa. It was his third time down the aisle and a number of people noticed he'd started to slow down a bit and spent more time at home. Still, there were those that thought his professional life was affecting him most. Nite saw it as well, though he pointed out that Myers was still capable of flashes of inspiration stating, "What I did was I kept in touch with him and when he went off to New York I had an opportunity to visit and say hello when I went over to WNEW. In 1967, I came out with an album on Laurie Records called *Rock and Roll: Evolution or Revolution*, a documentary. I went to see him over at WNEW and I gave him a copy, and he took it home and listened to it. I saw him the next day, and…he was the one who came up with this one phrase…he said, 'You know what? This is called a rockumentary!' *Record World* was doing a review of my album and they asked, 'What do you call it?' I said, 'A rockumentary' and the headline in that review asked, 'Are you ready for a rockumentary?' That phrase to this day is still used and it came from Pete Myers."

It wouldn't be the last time Nite had dealings with Pete Myers. He recalled a show he staged on May 5th, 1968 at the Cleveland Arena called "I Remember Rock and Roll", featuring Chuck Berry, Fats Domino, the Shirelles and the Coasters, all booked for just $7500. The show featured local disc jockeys as emcees, including Ken Hawkins from WJMO, WZAK's Dick Liberatore, and Jim LaBarbara and Joe Finan from WIXY. He also contacted Pete Myers who agreed to come in for what would be his final appearance in Cleveland. The ad for the concert listed all the jocks who would help emcee the event, but Myers' name isn't listed though it did promise "surprise guests".

LaBarbara remembers a lot more than just the greats who performed that night. "It was a crazy night. Fats Domino never showed up, and Chuck Berry had to do a double act that night. We were backstage and that's where I first met Mad Daddy. Pete Myers. I wasn't from Cleveland. I'm from Pittsburgh so I didn't know his whole story. Backstage, and then again at the cocktail party…there was an after party." LaBarbara would be overwhelmed by what was in store for himself, the other jocks and the audience.

Turns out Domino missed his plane, but that was only one of the major problems that evening. The Arena held 9500 but even at $3 a ticket the show only sold 1,250 seats. Everyone from the promoter's wife to Chuck Berry complained about the poor sound system with Berry saying, "The acoustics are terrible! No muffle. Everything bounces!" The show itself was solid despite the setbacks. The Shirelles took to the stage in silvery gowns, a little older and a little slower. Their dance steps were described as closer to "the Charleston instead of the Four Corners or the Funky Broadway", but those sparse crowds came for the hits and that's what they heard. "Mama Said", "Dedicated to the One I Love", "Will You Love Me Tomorrow". That gave way to the Coasters with only two of the original quartet but founding member Carl Gardner raced up to the stage calling out, "Feel like crackin' your fingers, go ahead!" The hits kept coming with "Charlie Brown" "Searchin", "Poison Ivy" and the rest of the catalog, and even a comedy skit with the singers portraying "Killer Joe", a clown and one dressed as a girl. Two acts were left…and one had yet to show. But the surprise guest took to the stage with a roar of excitement.

All the jocks got a great response but the lucky few at the show welcomed Pete Myers with a tidal wave of excitement. LaBarbara points out that even though Myers wasn't dressed as the Mad Daddy, he knew who he was as soon as he opened his mouth. "Pete Myers was dressed in khaki slacks, a blue blazer and a nice striped tie. And he had what we called back in the day a Princeton haircut, short and very nicely groomed. I never met Myers before that night, but I heard one of his airchecks. He was at my dream station, WNEW, where William B. Williams worked. He was a star!"

Thunderous applause shook the Arena and Myers seemed visibly moved. He didn't seem to expect the welcome and the other jocks looked on with great affection, and maybe a little bit of envy. But Mad Daddy had primed the crowd and it was time to bring out the big guns even if only one was in the wings.

There were 31 Cleveland policemen standing guard and while they didn't expect trouble, you could tell they sensed the surge of excitement as Chuck Berry took the stage. "Oh yeah!", he cried out, and the audience yelled back, "Yeah!" The seven amps on stage blared out the opening chords of "Nadine" and everyone was on their feet. The splits. the duck walk and, of course, hit after classic hit. "Memphis", Maybelline", songs he hadn't played in years, and then someone yelled, "Johnny B. Goode!" Chuck smiled and said, "That's closin'….and closin' is a long time away!" In reality, Berry was stalling for time because Fats Domino was a no show. His usual 45-minute act stretched to 80 minutes and the *Plain Dealer* claimed there was no extra charge. If that was the case it was a rare occasion because Berry was infamous for getting paid before he went on stage…in cash and put it in his briefcase that was near him as he played. Even so, Berry gave the audience what it came for, and after an exhausting set he wrapped it up at 8:45 by announcing, in song, that Fats Domino never arrived and, "Looks like it's the end of the show. Seems as though I have to go. I think there's something you ought to know…I'd like to leave you the way I found you, swinging!" He tore into the opening chords of "Johnny B. Goode" and left to an ovation that lasted ten minutes!

LaBarbara recalls with a smile, "It was interesting because Fats Domino did show up for that party and couldn't understand why nobody would talk to him. His band was there but Fats wasn't there for the show. He just walked around with no one to talk to." And then he got to observe Pete Myers as he made the rounds "Backstage he kept asking Joe Finan I bet three times, because Finan and I were talking about it later. Finan was on mornings, and I was doing nights at WIXY at that time. He kept asking, Are you happy? Are you happy you're back in Cleveland?' Joe was telling him, 'Yeah! It's great to be back. People remember me and all that.' That was pretty much the conversation. He kept asking, 'Are you happy? Are you happy?' If he asked it once he asked it three-four times. In reality, Myers might have benefited if he asked himself that very question.

Myers didn't want an appearance fee which could have cost Nite as much as $1000. The only compensation Myers asked for was a round trip airline ticket so he could return to New York that same night. Myers took the stage as Mad Daddy to a huge response from the audience. When the concert was over, Myers returned to his quiet introspective self, Nite drove him to the airport and the two parted ways.

Nite said he found Myers quiet demeanor puzzling, but at the same time understood the quiet side of his personality, and observed, "He was a performer doing his thing in a studio and on the radio, but when he was away from all that he was just a normal person. I guess that's what charges your battery and makes you go and do the things that you do because, again, it's very difficult for a person to be twenty-four hours a day doing the same thing. Being the person you are on-the-air and the same way off the air, because it has to burn you out real quick. You don't take that character home with you." Prior to his departure from the Arena, Myers did offer some comments to the *Plain Dealer* about the show stating, 'The acts are still great!", but questioned the scheduling of the concert saying. "This would have been better at Easter or Christmas vacation though." Myers also took the opportunity to compare the stars of the early days of rock and roll with the current artists of 1968. The *PD* quoted him as saying he "doesn't dig flower power" and that "many of the groups today aren't technically very good!" Keep in mind that at that point Myers was on easy listening WNEW / New York with another Cleveland favorite, Big Wilson.

The radio landscape changed drastically by autumn 1968. Broadcasters were now programming their FM bands separately, and a number staffed their stations with young, often inexperienced disc jockeys playing progressive rock. With all the freedom on those stations, to a great degree because they had problems selling advertising on those new untested formats, the programming on the AM airwaves was much tighter. Program directors forced adherence to show clocks that required a number of songs per hour, along with promotions and commercials, and that left little time or freedom for air personalities to be heard. Some described the lack of freedom as leaving them "professionally impotent."

Pete Myers had accepted his position at WNEW. Perhaps he was forced to, but still seemed comfortable with a secure job in the midday 1 to 4 p.m. shift. But the old saying in radio even back then was, the only constant is change. Change was on the way that first week of October 1968.

Myers was told by management that he was to be given a later shift, from 8 p.m. to midnight. He would start the new shift on Friday, October 4. Station officials would later say Myers accepted the change with a smile and even seemed enthusiastic about the new time slot.

It was early fall. When you think back to October 4th of that year you saw a lot of tension in Manhattan, and the whole U.S. The Soviet Foreign Minister Andrei Gromyko was at the United Nations stating his country was all for disarmament and arms control, but the occupation of Czechoslovakia would continue. There was a presidential race, too. Lyndon Johnson was finishing out his term, and his administration held firm on legislation that blocked anti-integration efforts in segregated schools. A few blocks away from the White House the Yippie leader Abbie Hoffman was arrested for wearing a shirt made from an American flag when he tried to barge into a hearing for the House Un-American Activities Committee.

Oh, and a third-party candidate…Alabama governor George Wallace…had picked a running mate, General Curtis LeMay. At one time he served as the Air Force Chief of Staff and went on record right from the start saying he would approve of the use of nuclear weapons in VietNam "if necessary", but also stated, "I'll be damn lucky if I don't appear as a drooling idiot whose only solution to any problem is to drop atomic bombs!" The GOP's flag bearer Richard Nixon told a Southern TV audience that Wallace didn't deserve to president, and Democratic candidate vice president Hubert Humphrey told campaign crowds, "I wouldn't trust the Republican party with a piggy bank!" New York school teachers were poised to strike, police clashed with rock throwing students at Seward Park High School, and the Neighborhood Youth Corps was investigating a massive embezzlement scandal. Stuff like that was happening in cities across the country. It was so prevalent the country became almost numb to those reports.

Even so, that Friday was a nice day in New York. A little sunshine and a light breeze. It was the kind of day where you might walk out, look around, take a deep breath and think what a great day to be alive. Something was about to happen at 370 East 76th Street. That morning, Myers dressed in his best suit, and said goodbye to his wife who was just waking up. Lisa Myers would later remember how elegant Pete looked that day. He excused himself and walked into the bathroom where he had placed one of his most prized possessions, a rare and valuable 12-guage shotgun. Moments later, just before 9 a.m., a shot rang out and Lisa Myers found her husband dead by his own hand. A rifle blast to the chest.

There was a suicide note nearby. We tried to track it down through the New York police, but over the years it was apparently misplaced in the room where they stored evidence. It reportedly stated Myers was despondent over the change in his shift and the direction of his career. WNEW's general manager, David Croninger, issued a statement saying, "All of us are deeply disturbed at Peter's death. He must rank as one of the best in the business, bringing a professionalism not often found. He will be missed by those of us at WNEW who worked with him and by his many listeners." The president of Metromedia which owned WNEW, John Van Buren Sullivan, added to those comments stating, "Pete Myers was a man worth knowing. He was an expert in his profession because he worked hard and cared about people".

There is another unsettling aspect regarding Myers' death, a legend that is whispered among his fans concerning his final moments before his sudden departure. While it is was reported that he dressed in a suit and left a note, the story has been often repeated that Myers was listening to a tape of the Mad Daddy when his final moment came. The origin of that point in this story can't be verified though it has been passed on as part of his legend since that fateful day. His radio colleagues heard that same report, but it should be stressed that no official record exists of that aspect of his demise. Still, the story persists, however until some solid verification is revealed…and at this late stage that seems very unlikely…we should consider it an urban legend. Myers had the ability with his home equipment, but the proof of this morbid footnote just doesn't exist.

Jim La Barbara recalls the shock of hearing about Myers death, especially in light of seeing him in such good spirits when they shared the stage the Cleveland Arena. "It was a very nice, very casual atmosphere back there. Then about five months later I'm on the air at WIXY and I remember reading the story on the air, 'Yesterday, a former Cleveland disc jockey and WNEW personality 40-year-old Pete Myers died of an apparent suicide." The station owner Norman Wain, called me in shock that he had died. At that time, he was married to a young lady who was a model. A lot younger than him and a really good-looking New York model. He had everything in the world to be happy about. He's in New York. He's on WNEW!" LaBarbara also echoed the long standing rumor about Myers' final moments, saying ,"I don't know how true the story was but I heard it many times. He apparently walked into the bathroom with his favorite shotgun and committed suicide listening to some old Mad Daddy tapes. He left a note saying he was despondent because he was on his afternoon show 1 to 4 and then he went to the 8 to midnight show. I was shocked when I read it on the air and then when Norman called and said, 'I knew him so well!" But it wasn't the last time LaBarbara would hear about Myers.

"Fast forward and I'm at WLW (Cincinnati). Our new midnight guy was Chuck Dougherty from Philadelphia, but he had been in New York. We were talking one day and somehow, we started talking about Mad Daddy." The guy known as "Chucky from Kentucky" had quite a resume. He helped launch the famed KQV Top 40 format and did tours of duty in some major markets, including a legendary stint doing morning drive in Pittsburgh before heading to the Big Apple. As La Barbara recalls," Dougherty told me when he was hired in New York he was the one who got Pete Myers shift at WNEW moving Myers to 8 to midnight. He didn't know Myers that well, but when he committed suicide he said, 'That's it. I'm gone. There's no hope for me at this station!' He was only there a short time after that, resigned and went back to Philadelphia."

Myers' brother Ernie recalled that Pete was "very depressed when the station changed his shift." and his former producer and program director Neil McIntyre believed Myers' profound interest in eastern culture as well as his avid interest in guns may have led him to commit a form of "Hari Kari", or ritual suicide by honor. Norm N. Nite claimed that was a distinct possibility, saying, "Who knows? There were many sides to him, more than just being the character of 'Mad Daddy.' He had a knowledge of all kinds of music. He liked the big band era, and he was a trained actor. A man who has all this going for him…there were many spokes in the wheel, but we just knew one spoke and that was him being Pete Myers and 'Mad Daddy.' There were other sides to him, and unless you were real close to him, you didn't know the other sides." Few people, if any, did. Word of Myers' death got back to his old roommates who sadly took it in stride. Travis Roudebush would say, " I remember when I heard he died…and was I surprised? No, not really. He was always a crazy spur of the moment guy."

There was a memorial less than 48 hours later at a funeral home at Madison Avenue and East 81st Street. His death affected fans in New York as well as Cleveland. Walt Sabo was one of them, "I knew when he killed himself, newsman Edward Brown did a stunning eulogy to him. We had to do a project for my English class, and I did it on that eulogy." But Sabo says the reasons for Myers decision may have been a combination of reasons. "When he died, he also had gambling debts and his income in voice over work was going to be cut when he moved to nights. He would be a less appealing commercial voice actor. I think the suicide was a combination of doing nights in the radio slum of 8 to midnight, the cut in VO work, gambling debts, going to Cleveland that month and being reminded of what he had been. That's a lot."

Jay Hunt agrees Myers' failure to make Mad Daddy a hit to a bigger audience weighed heavily on him, and by no real fault of his own. Hunt said, "In the end, it was the changing music scene that killed off Mad Daddy. By 1960 original rock and roll was dead replaced by phonies like 'Bobby This' and 'Bobby That', Fabian and even fake groups like The Monkees. It's no wonder that the next great innovations came out of Britain, not the U.S." Brother Ernie added a postscript stating, "Cleveland might have played a role. He wanted the recognition, to make Mad Daddy a star. It didn't work in New York, but when he went back, he realized he left everything he ever wanted in Cleveland."

Years later, Ernie Anderson would say he still thought about Pete Myers claiming, "He was a brilliant, sensitive, lonely man, but I think his brilliance killed him."

Chapter Nine

What is a Fisteris?

In its own way imitation is a form of paying tribute to someone who broke new ground with their incomparable originality and Myers certainly laid the groundwork for the rapid fire air personalities that followed him for decades after. John Larsh, better known as "Yo' leader!'" Big Jack Armstrong would certainly fit that category during his near fifty-year run-on pop music stations across the country. Larsh's energy was infectious and while he never outright copied Myers, whom he might have never heard, he recognized the power of the medium on a young, focused audience that Mad Daddy knew from the start. There were others, including Scott Howitt whose rhyming patter paid tribute to Myers years later with a retro delivery that reached out to the oldies format audience that grew up with Daddy and transported them to a different time in their lives. Coincidentally, both Larsh and Howitt got their big breaks in Cleveland radio where Myers had his greatest success. Yet another Cleveland radio pioneer, Billy Bass, an alumnus of Larsh's former station WIXY-AM as well as Howitt's WMJI-FM, cites Myers as a great influence and entertainer. As Bass tells it, 'I was a huge fan of Mad Daddy. The music played on his show and his act was extremely entertaining He was so cool, so off beat, so hip.... I had never heard anything like him on the radio. He was the kind of guy that I hoped to meet but never did.... I could listen to him for hours; it was that much fun." Bass would go on to become one of the founding fathers of Cleveland's FM rock radio breaking new ground at the start up WMMS-FM in 1968 (for two tours of duty) and WNCR-FM breaking artists such as David Bowie, Pacific Gas and Electric and a long list of acts that achieved superstar status. Yet another Cleveland FM pioneer, Steve "Doc Nemo" Nemeth… a veteran of the original progressive format on WMMS-FM and WIXY-AM as well as earlier experiments on the city's ethnic stations…describes Mad Daddy in the most affectionate terms as an "iconoclast". "There was no one like him", Nemeth says. "No one could be like him. He was that original, that harmonic convergence of talent, incentive and attitude that you rarely experience and to hear him do it night after night was amazing. He was the right mix…of anarchy and entertainment!" Future radio personality Len Anthony also cited Myers influence in an article about the then teenager's radio aspirations in 1964.

Kurt Vonnegut once wrote in a foreword for a book about comedians Bob Elliot and Ray Goulding that, "It is the truth: Comedians and jazz musicians have been more comforting and enlightening to me than preachers or politicians or philosophers or poets or painters or novelists of my time. Historians, in the future, in my opinion, will congratulate us on very little other than our clowning and our jazz."

If that is indeed the case, Pete "Mad Daddy" Myers will likely be treated kindly by those historians, not only for his taste in roots rhythm and blues music but also for the unique style of entertainment he pioneered with his alter-ego. That is, if he's remembered at all.

Myers was still very much on people's minds in the months after his death. It was reported that a year almost to the day after his death actor Soupy Sales was being considered for a role as TV idol Mad Daddy in the screen version of Rona Jaffe's book, <u>The Fame Game</u>. This is especially ironic because Sales… like Alan Freed and Myers…had also worked at Cleveland's WJW as Soupy Hines in the early 1950s. Still despite recent interest in the alternative press and a career retrospective issued by the New York based Norton Records, Pete "Mad Daddy" Myers is mostly remembered by radio historians and his many fans in Northeast Ohio and New York City. Norm N. Nite observed accessibility may be the reason. "His stint here in Cleveland was so brief, and the same thing with the shows. When he was on in the evening, kids at that time were out riding around in cars and listening. They weren't home. If you had a

Webcor or one of those big bulky tape recorders of that time, you're still not going to stay home in the evening. You're going to be out with your friends. How are you going to record him? That's why there are so few tapes of him. But again, some things have surfaced and there are things that you find out from other people. This guy might have recorded a couple of hours, this guy a couple of hours. Slowly but surely, you're finding material out there."

How did the transition from radio to TV affect Myers? Was it a smaller audience that increased his popularity? Myers' historian Jay Hunt doesn't believe he ever directly considered this issue. "He was simply one of the 'cult personality deejays' typical of the early rock and roll era. Their presence on the airwaves helped to define radio's new role as primarily a deliverer of pop music rather than its radio theatre of the air past."

It's evident that Myers' Mad Daddy brought in a large and loyal audience to his Cleveland radio show but could not duplicate that anywhere else. Even though he was wildly successful on Cleveland radio, his role in that transition was limited to Northeast Ohio. Some disc jockeys, like Bill Randle at WERE / Cleveland, were able to expand their base of influence. Randle worked in both Cleveland and New York City, splitting his time between the two cities during the week at the height of his popularity as a disc jockey. But Randle's on-air presentation was more direct and truer to his own character as a straight-talking air personality. Randle's personality was also a suitable fit for the radio formats he worked in. Pete Myers had success as Mad Daddy with WJW and WHK's rock and roll format in Cleveland, but it was a disaster on middle-of-the-road WINS in New York. He would have likely had a greater role in that transition if Mad Daddy had been placed in a rock and roll format right from the start in New York City.

Myers also used a bizarre alter ego. He created a character that appealed to the young audience sought by radio programmers battling TV for advertising dollars. Plus, the post-World War II generation found itself the focus of marketers promoting music, clothing and other considerations to a large group of young people who were mobile with their own cars and often had expendable cash. It was the first time that an entire generation was being targeted by marketers differently than their parents. Myers could deliver that audience in Northeast Ohio, but you can make an argument that Myers ambitions for a larger radio market and the failure of programmers in New York to recognize and successfully exploit his talents and personality limited the role he could have played in that transition.

While John Zacherle at WCAU-AM in Philadelphia had a similar though less frantic gothic style character on-air, he did not have the same wide appeal as "Mad Daddy" in Cleveland. In addition, the purchase of that station by the much more traditional CBS radio network forced Zacherle to find work elsewhere. He was able to revive the character, now known as "Zacherley", hosting a late-night Friday horror movie on WABC-TV. But Zacherley's airtime was limited, and he played to a niche audience on TV once a week. Myers' "Mad Daddy" was prime time in a format that didn't fit the character playing to an older radio audience in the most important media market in the world. Plus, his attempts to sell the character in syndication met with little success. There was no other major radio market that showed a character with the same appeal and popularity that Myers' "Mad Daddy" had in Cleveland. That indicated Cleveland was unique in embracing Myers' character, which failed to make an impact and influence anywhere else. Myers was able to hold his radio audience from going to television, but his influence was confined to Northeast Ohio.

But what was Myers' incentive to even invent Mad Daddy? Pop culture, especially satirical magazines like *Mad* and sweeping changes in the musical landscape, reflected the increasingly free lifestyle of the nation's youth. Myers told WZAK's Dick Liberatore in their 1967 interview that he came up with the Mad Daddy character while sitting at the WHKK / Akron transmitter site. It leads one to believe that Mad Daddy was the brainchild of a creative individual inspired by the new media but frustrated by boredom and his own stalled incentive. Jay Hunt offered this assessment.

"Who knows what drove him to become Mad Daddy? He seems to have always been a prankster at heart as evidenced by his 'Monster from the Sea' while in the service and his Joker record. I believe he originated an early form of his Mad Daddy format on WHKK / Akron, possibly drawing from early horror film hosts on TV but more likely from *Mad* magazine." The rhyming patter was original although he may have seen it in comics like Basil Wolverton's *Powerhouse Pepper*.

This observation provides a key link to Mad Daddy's on-air personae. Wolverton was a regular contributor and artist for *Mad*. His *Powerhouse Pepper* was a strip based on a wise cracking strong man published as a separate comic book in Timely Comics between 1942 and 1948. Timely also included Wolverton's *Scoop Scuttle* as back stories in its *Daredevil and Silver Streak* titles, and the characters in the strip spoke in the same whimsical syncopated rhyme scheme that Mad Daddy later adopted into his own rapid-fire delivery. Myers was a regular reader of *Mad* magazine which included Wolverton's work, even having a letter published in one of its issues in the 1950s. In an obvious move aimed at self-promotion, it read, "As a long-time fan of *Mad*, I was nuts enough to be the first deejay to play your new *Fink Along with Mad* album. By the way, the record makes a terrific flying saucer. I found that out when our Program Director ripped it off the turntable, ran to the nearest open window, and skimmed it across Central Park. Some guys just aren't as 'mad' as others!" and he signed it, "Pete Myers, WINS Radio, New York City." This would show *Mad*'s likely influence on Myers' Mad Daddy, as well as the emerging baby boomer generation. Myers wasn't the only member of that counter-culture vanguard to reflect *Mad*'s irreverent look at life in the mid-20th century. The magazine may have hit its peak in the Sixties when Mick Jagger and Jimi Hendrix were photographed scanning its pages. The Beatles were also fans of comic books and Alfred E. Neuman's musings with

Ringo immortalized in a classic ad parody for "Blecch Shampoo" painted by the legendary pop culture illustrator Frank Frazetta. In its early days as it rapidly evolved from a comic book with *Tales Calculated to Drive You MAD* to the magazine aimed at putting a burr under the saddle of conservative post-war America, *Mad* was a sounding board for a generation ready to cast off conformity and Pete Myers was happy to take that message to his audience.

While Mad Daddy took this to a new often extreme level, WHKK / Akron was able to sell critical advertising time on his show. The "Mad Daddy" may have been completely out of character with other members of the air staff, but as long as he generated revenue the station programmers allowed him free reign. Myers enjoyed that free reign with a one-man show, and as long as it brought in ratings and advertising dollars there was no reason to change. Mad Daddy was a combination of popular culture influences from print, film, recorded music and Myers' own fertile imagination. They were the same influences embraced by much of the emerging youth culture that was now being targeted by advertisers and marketing concerns as a separate generation from their parents. Plus, he was willing to take his character to extremes.

It should also be stressed that while Myers left a sizable audio imprint on the history of radio, it was his lasting influence on his audience that may be his greatest achievement. Jim Kolar was in his early teens when the Mad Daddy reigned on Cleveland's airwaves, and he recalls Myers crossing entertainment's racial barrier during radio's "Pat Boone Era". Like his predecessor Alan Freed, Myers stressed the importance of roots music and artists, but was quick to point out that harmony could be achieved socially as well as artistically. "He loved a group called The Crests", according to Kolar, "and '16 Candles' was a staple on Daddy's show when it was climbing up the charts. Mad Daddy loved black music. Lots of us did. Great music didn't have a color, but Mad Daddy pointed out in his own unique way… that The Crests were a racially integrated doo-wop group." The group was also a favorite of Dick Clark who gave them plenty of TV time and, as Kolar points out, the lead singer Johnny Maestro went on to score a huge hit years later as a member of The Brooklyn Bridge with "The Worst That Could Happen".

Bob Mokus has stories as well. As a kid in the 1950s he was weaned on many of the greats on the Cleveland radio dial. Mokus recalls the importance of his radio favorites Bill Randle (who essentially broke Elvis Presley as a rock and roller north of the Mason-Dixon line) and Phil McLean on WERE-AM, though he wasn't afraid to check out Cleveland's KYW-AM and Nashville's WLAC-AM, and later WHK's Johnny Holliday. Mokus recalls that, "I and some of my friends were regular Mad Daddy listeners and fans during the 1958-59 period. We first heard him on WJW…I guess right around the time that he was also doing the Channel 8 weekend movie bit…and followed him to WHK." Now, keep in mind that this was an era when disc jockeys…like the early rock and roll stars…were strongly encouraged to get out on the road and meet their audience. It could generate a lot of income along with promotion, and a young Pete Myers was up to the challenge…as long as he could do it in the guise of Mad Daddy. Mokus was lucky enough to see that first-hand on two different occasions. It was also a time when radio personalities from competing stations could share a stage to reach a common audience.

The memory of that first encounter is burned into Mokus' memory, saying "Sometime in November 1958 after he'd started at WHK, Pete made one of his out-of-town personal appearances in my hometown of Wooster, which is about fifty miles south of Cleveland, as special guest DJ at the weekly Saturday night record hop at the nearby National Guard Armory on U.S. route 30. I was 15, and as next-door-neighbor to one of the veterans who organized the events I was privileged to help run the refreshment stand every week. Surrounded by a couple hundred happy attendees that particular evening I did have the opportunity to approach all of the visiting 'celebs' for greetings and autographs." It was a meeting that would have a far lasting impact on the young fan. He adds that,

"Local WWST Wooster radio personalities rotated as DJ hosts from week-to-week, which that Saturday meant Bill Ridenour…prior to his later upward career moves to WHLO-AM in Akron and WLW-AM / Cincinnati. The headliner that night was Little Anthony and the Imperials. "'Little Anthony' Gourdine and one of the other Imperials came down with Pete to lip-synch not only their recent debut hit 'Tears On My Pillow' but also their brand-new single release…which got stuck in the groove and began repeating itself during the performance!" But the real star was waiting in the wings.

"Pete was garbed in his black cape costume, as was his lady assistant who signed her name 'Mad Momma'", though Mokus is quick to add that he didn't know who she was in real-life. "I've found it interesting that his handout publicity photo had never been very gracefully altered to reflect the apparent spelling change of his professional name from 'Meyers' to 'Myers,' so the letter 'e' had just been blacked out." Mokus points out that Myers was credited with the spelling "Meyers" on his G & F record release "What is a Fisteris?" b/w "The Joker" back in 1958. He also notes that the instrumental backing for "Fisteris" is Chuck Berry's "Blue Feeling" which was the flip side of "Rock and Roll Music" in 1956. Myers had another impact on Mokus' life. "My best friend during early high school years was the son of the owner of the Wooster Music Center, where most everyone in town bought their records, musical instruments, and other audio equipment. In 1958, he brought home his very own reel-to-reel tape recorder, which enthralled me! After we had spent many sessions exploring its wonderful possibilities, I decided that I just had to have one for myself…which is why I entered Mad Daddy's weekly WHK contest from which you could win a tape recorder for correctly predicting the following week's top five record hits. As a real pop music geek (largely from years of listening to Bill Randle on WERE), I sent in my entry, and…to my joy and surprise…heard Pete announce my name as a winner! Only much later did my father reveal that this incident had changed his plans to buy me a tape machine that Christmas." It changed other plans as well. As Mokus tells it, after a stint at Kent State University, he was drafted in 1967 and upon his return, "opted for radio jobs without ever returning to higher education (which was a bit of a disappointment to my college professor father)."

Tom Pope cites Myers' influence as well. Another Cleveland fan, Pope is now based in California but still sees the impact Myers made as Mad Daddy to a young and impressionable post WWII audience saying, "Cleveland was a steel town where we responded to the industrial-strength rhythms of factory work. That music was rooted in rhythm and blues and it inspired glimmers of integration, a concept our parents feared, as it seemingly went against their natural order. DJs like Alan Freed and Bill Randle blazed the biracial trail that Mad Daddy so supremely celebrated, putting the outrageous verbal bebop of Lord Buckley's black oratory on the air, becoming Cleveland's ultimate hipster". Pope doesn't recall what brought him to the Mad Daddy show, though it may have been like a lot of young fans just skimming the dial and hearing his one of a kind delivery or his theme, Andre Williams' "Greasy Chicken". And, like Bob Mokus, Pope was one of the lucky listeners who actually met the mysterious Mad Daddy. "Seemed like a nice guy. I was in a crowd of his fans at the Immaculate Conception Lawn Fete. His wife made the strongest impression, long, golden hair and a lavender dress. More uptown than Willoughby, Ohio, was used to. I remember her as beautiful, but I was in my early teens and my prefrontal cortex was just getting started. Even so, Mad Daddy was the main attraction. Pope tell us his act reflected the changes in entertainment targeting the emerging post war culture "influenced by the new style of humor and parody of the 1950s focused on a young audience. *Mad* magazine. Sheb Wooley with "The Purple People Eater". David Seville's "Witch Doctor", and Screamin' Jay Hawkins' performances, Buchanan and Goodman with the cut-in records, and so on." Again, he points to similarities with Lord Buckley stating, "Buckley was the father of modern comedy, an outrageous storyteller using the language slaves used to keep their meaning from the 'master.' He called it the Zig Zag semantic. Quincy Jones considers him the 'original rapper.' He's where Mad Daddy's madness came from… the irresistible allure of the hip." That semantic seems to reflect on what was then the modern audience with pope indicating, "Young people had their own music, music their parents didn't like and were scornful of. Sinatra tried the genre but failed. He was the older generation, square, not hip. Like Alan Freed, Mad Daddy played R & B songs by the original artists (not Pat Boone remakes). In a racist America was that an attraction to youth? A "forbidden fruit" for the sons and daughters of a largely racially divided America?" The point is also made that Myers was a man before his time and could have used the emerging technology of the day more effectively. "I think he would have grown considerably on FM radio, but that wouldn't happen for another eight years with Tom Donahue on KSAN in San Francisco. TV offered an obviously bigger future. Lord Buckley's peers were Red Skelton and Milton Berle, who parlayed their radio shows into popular early TV shows. Buckley was a frequent guest on Ed Sullivan's really big show." Mad Daddy's one-month run was a taste of things to come, but one that frustrated him early on as he abandoned the local TV format.

Another aspect to Mad Daddy's continuing legend is the scarcity of recorded work. As Pope mentions, "The myth grows when there is little to show" citing the legend of blues master Robert Johnson based on a handful of recordings and just three known photos. Will future generations remember Pete "Mad Daddy" Myers? Pope believes, "People will have to be reminded. Few people other than comedians know Lord Buckley, but occasionally he'll surface, and eventually a movie or doc will be made. So, 'hang loose Mother Goose, let the mellow jello flow'. Mad Daddy was Cleveland's ultimate hipster".

Myers' self-promotion both on and off the air is well documented. As Norm N. Nite stated, "He was a performer. Bailing out of a plane when his contract was up. He was so far ahead of his time with the things that he did and thought about. Absolutely amazing." Myers also was one of the first local on-air personalities to do self-marketing with his attempts at syndication deals, and products like batty bucks shoes. It's hard to find any other radio personality that took self-promotion to the extremes pursued by Pete Myers. Keep in mind that Myers also pursued the parachute jump when he was between stations. It is unlikely that any other station would have assumed the liability and risk of having one of its employees risk their lives in a stunt that could have easily turned tragic. In addition, Cleveland was always a breakout market for artists as well as a training ground for up-and-coming radio personalities. Still, Pete Myers' Mad Daddy failed to get the same reaction in New York as in Cleveland. Jim Jaworski said, "The Cleveland fans were ahead of all the other fans in accepting rock and roll. New York was behind the loop. They probably got scared of him. They didn't know how to handle him."

There's likely another reason and that was the New York talent. Walt Sabo believes, "A key factor to his failure as a top 40 jock in New York City is that, like Cleveland if he had replaced Alan Freed in New York, it might have worked. But in New York he had competing manic jocks such as B. Mitchel Reed on WMCA who out screamed and outweirded him and Bruce Morrow on WABC who had more energy and more sincerity. Murray the K had put that type of energy on WINS prior to Pete so the landscape was different. Also. New Yorkers as a rule have liked eccentrics but have never responded to pure schtick."

That same position is echoed by noted broadcast historian Dr. Rich Klein, formerly with Cleveland State University. He was fortunate to have experienced Mad Daddy both in Cleveland and the New York radio markets, and he believes, "the sense of freedom he displayed nightly may have contributed to his undoing. He was so far ahead of his times. Mad Daddy was Lenny Bruce, George Carlin and Alfred E. Newman all rolled into one with a dash of Boris Karloff and Bela Lugosi for good measure. Over time, he may have become frustrated when the world around him did not keep up with him. He might have liked others emulating him, or perhaps it scared him. He also might have wondered what to do next if he was no longer the leader in the block of the 'cool' kids. As you know DJ's egos sometimes get the best of them and that might have been his case. We will never know for sure. However, one thing I can say for sure is that I always knew that fun was just around the corner when I heard the WINS announcer say that 'from around the corner and down the block it's time for the *Mad Daddy Show.*'"

Greg Miller said the New York programmers also may not have understood Myers' act or the audience he appealed to. "I don't know that he was on the right station. They weren't ready for him. He was also one of the first late night TV movie hosts. In the late 1950s you had these late-night movie hosts, and Pete Myers made that transition. It was a double feature on Friday nights, and he had the same schtick…the cape and the pancake makeup, and he hosted the movie. That never took off, but when you look at the phenomena that started here in Cleveland with Ernie Anderson and Ghoulardi, and so on, it's a genre that always seemed to find a home here in Cleveland."

Miller said Cleveland TV, as in the case of New York's radio programmers, may not have been ready at the time to exploit Mad Daddy's true appeal. Ernie Anderson's Ghoulardi was a local television phenomenon due in great part to Anderson marketing the character himself through personal appearances. Anderson also knew when and how to leave and, in the process, left a legend and even some imitators.

Ernie Myers visited Pete in New York and sat in on his show during his WINS days. There was a heavy teen audience, but nowhere near the numbers seen in Cleveland. Ernie Myers said no one influenced Pete as Mad Daddy was completely original. He played as others have suggested a sort of gothic beatnik, and his character was so unique it would be painfully evident if someone did try to imitate him or duplicate Mad Daddy. But a continuing influence doesn't necessarily mean imitation.

Norm N. Nite pointed out that influence could be on the audience level as well. As Nite stated, "People who cherish that era of rock and roll, and he was at rock and roll's peak in '58 and '59 in Cleveland, for him to be able to come in at that particular time and be able to do the things that he was doing and make an impact…. The people who grew up in that era and all the songs that came out at that particular time are real treasures as far as the history of rock and roll goes. For him, with all the disc jockeys that were out there, to make an impact on teenagers was remarkable."

But Nite pointed out there were still a lot of people who tried to emulate rather than imitate him, saying, "There were disc jockeys who wanted to go for the rhyming thing like Scott Howitt on 'Majic' (WMJI-FM). There was another guy who was imitating him and sounded just like him, and who knows how many others that we don't know about that tried to do the same thing?" Former Myers roommate Travis Roudebush adds, "I remember when I first saw Ghoulardi, and I thought it was Mad Daddy all over again. Let's say he 'borrowed' a lot of stuff from Pete Myers." It should also be stressed that Ernie Anderson's Ghoulardi was an original character, though he may have been subliminally affected by some of Pete Myers style. Both were unique characters, and each had styles that would be hard if not impossible to duplicate.

Greg Miller agreed saying there were imitators who could not match Myers' innovative style as Mad Daddy. "I think there were a lot of deejays in the early sixties that tried to copy that style. Jack Armstrong, the 'Wild Child' at WIXY. I think that he was back in an age when the deejays had a lot more power and a lot more latitude in what they could do. I know Ghoulardi, Ernie Anderson, was influenced by him. That whole late night horror movie genre was from him."

Miller went on to say, "He had his own unique style, but as far as that frenetic delivery…unscripted…nobody could match Pete Myers. Nobody. What he was doing was true artistry, where he could just recite stuff off the top of his head and make it flow with the rhythm and just lead it into a record, and with music of different genres combining jazz, rock and roll and offbeat beatnik sounds.

They had a freewheeling free flow kind of stream of consciousness thing."

Nite also stressed the uniqueness of Myers' style and personality. Nite remembered his last meeting with Myers at the Cleveland Arena in 1968, and how it may have affected him to see the influence he still had on an audience he left nine years before. "What happened was he was there and everyone loved him, and then he went back to New York. On October 4th of '68 is when he committed suicide. Over the years I just thought he was ahead of his time, the way he did what he did, the rhyming…he was just so good and clever and quick and everything else. I never saw anyone else who was able to do the things that he was able to do."

Jay Hunt had a different idea. "I wouldn't say he was ahead of his time because that would mean that others had followed in his footsteps doing the same thing. I'd say he was like none other in his time. He was truly unique and totally in tune with his teen audience of the day."

One of Myers' lasting influences that might be overlooked by so called mainstream audiences, and definitely should not, is his impact on the evolution of what's commonly called "psychobilly" music which, like its less melodic cousin punk, threw off the restraints of traditional pop and comes at you like an audio hurricane. Researcher David Ensminger quotes noted radio host Count Reeshard's assessment of Myer's final appearance on WHK as a prime example of Mad Daddy's freedom with a show, "awash in sound effects, maniacal laughter, tons of runaway repeat – echo, all to the accompaniment of many, many greasy rock and roll and rhythm and blues 45's". He points out that Myers' created a sound "unencumbered by some draconian station format" and crossing musical genres including black and Hispanic musicians that drew deep concern from lily-white (okay, lets call it what it was "racist America") but was "manna for Mad Daddy". A similar sentiment was expressed by the Dead Boys' Jimmy Zero commenting on Myers' former newsman Ernie Anderson's alter ego, Ghoulardi, who became an overnight superstar in the 1960s on Cleveland TV's "Shock Theater". Zero mentioned that punk, like Ghoulardi, and as echoed by Steve "Doc Nemo" Nemeth, showed that "anarchy can be entertainment".

Myers' influence also manifested itself in a way that neither he nor anyone else could have foreseen during his lifetime. While he did have an influence on Ernie Anderson's Ghoulardi on WJW-TV, Myers also influenced punk rock pioneer Lux Interior of the band The Cramps. Born Erick Lee Purkhiser in Stow, Ohio, he developed his band's "psycho-billy" sound based on the free-form horror and exploitation movies shown on Mad Daddy and Ghoulardi's TV programs as well as the free-wheeling controlled chaos heard on Myers' radio shows. He also proudly owned a promotional photo of Mad Daddy inscribed "To Eric". As *Plain Dealer* writer John Petkovic wrote in Lux Interior's obituary profile in February 2009, "Their mix of hip, beatnik rapping, raunchy blues tunes and 'so bad it's good' sensibilities provided the template for the band's sound."

The Cramps also recorded a tribute to Myers' in the song *Mad Daddy* on the album *Songs the Lord Taught Us* (A&M,1980). Included in the lyrics were the words,

"Pair of shades. Purple shoes. I got a parachute to land on you."

The last line would seem to be a reference to Myers' promotional jump from a plane in Lake Erie, as well as his "batty bucks" shoes. Myers' memory was obviously held dearly by a number of creative and influential performers, as well as many of his aging fans who heard him during his heyday in Cleveland.

Even so, on a much larger scale, Pete Myers is remembered today as an odd postscript in broadcasting history, though a loyal group of fans still keep his memory alive. Jay Hunt is one of them and said, "Overall deejays like him were a dying breed in the new format-oriented radio. Just like rock and roll, by the early sixties radio had lost much of the individuality that fifties generational rebellion had fostered. White backlash against black music, the payola scandal and Tin Pan Alley re-establishing its control over the music industry were all factors in bringing both down. A few like the

Cramps tried to keep him alive, but sadly he is mostly remembered nostalgically by old folks like me."

Pete Myers' was said to be so troubled by the change in his shift that he decided death was a better alternative. But even he realized that change is inevitable, telling WZAK's Dick Liberatore that it was evident in the world of popular music. Myers told him, "There's an old saying 'there's nothing new under the sun' and I think that's very true because nothing seems so constant as change. Yet all the changes seem to come back to the same old thing. There's a real earthy gut bucket beat to it and there's twelve bar blues and by me it's going to be 'mellow jello' in 1987 every time I hear a new record with a new group. The names are getting wilder, that's all I know. I hear Dow Jones and the Averages. Six and the Single Girl. That's another group. I used to think the wildest name for a group would be the Foregone Conclusions. Now there is the Foregone Conclusions, but I don't know where they are on the charts. But they're all singing twelve bar blues and it still goes the same way." It's also evident that opting to end his life may have been a spur of the moment decision because we hear from that interview done before Myers' death that he was thinking about what his life would be like twenty years in the future in 1987.

It was an era when his fans would listen from car radios or transistor sets hidden under a pillow after bedtime to hear Mad Daddy say good night in a way that might have been used to eulogize him when he chose to end his own life.

No more time to rhyme and shout.

Daddy disappears! The winking eye goes out!

Brush your teeth and say your prayers.

Cha-cha softly up the stairs.

Remember your Daddy loves you! Pleasant dreams.

See you tomorrow…in the land of screams!

Just the beat of my heart…in the dark.

A CD career retrospective, magazine and newspaper articles, songs such as the Cramps' "Mad Daddy" and even cell phone ring tones recall a much simpler and more creative time in Cleveland radio. They also reveal an individual who was so wildly creative that certain radio programmers and marketing people didn't know how to exploit his character to its maximum potential.

Radio needed unique personalities and programming to draw and keep young listeners in the 1950s and 60s who might be lured away by the increasing popularity of television. The industry was in need of new creative ideas and personalities that could sell themselves as entertainment as well as the music they played. There were no limits, but no one anticipated the degree that Pete Myers would take his imagination. As the radio programmers in Cleveland had hoped, the Mad Daddy became an immediate hit with his young audience, presenting music and live entertainment that was radically different from any other station. Pete Myers' Mad Daddy character was embraced by listeners on WJW-AM and later WHK-AM, and he could have remained very comfortable at WHK though his own ambition compelled Myers to take his creation to a bigger radio market. When the character was introduced and quickly failed on New York City's middle-of-the-road WNEW, Myers faced what appeared to be his first major career failure. He struggled to reintroduce the character in syndication and on commercial radio, but never achieved the same success he saw in Cleveland. Shortly after his final visit to Cleveland, perhaps frustrated that he could not duplicate his fame in Northeast Ohio, Myers took his own life. New York newspaper columnist David Hinckley suggests Myer's suicide may have added to his legend because his career "was so short and ended so badly." As Hinckley notes during Myers last stand as Daddy at WINS, "The times were a-changin', though also was the music, and the magic had dimmed."

Years later, Myers' legacy was still being debated. People had a hard time figuring him out even when he was still with us. "The Big Chief", the late Norman Wain, knew Myers and his formidable talents. "He was two different people! I met Pete Myers, and he was tough to read. He was pleasant enough and quiet, even more so than that "lovable laughable" tag they gave him and a far cry from Mad Daddy. You heard the two on the radio and had to think, 'How does he do it!?' It's like he flipped some sort of switch in his brain! When he did the show at night, he talked faster than an auctioneer. It was all off the top of his head. I would have loved to have him on WIXY but he was long gone to New York by then. (Wain started WIXY-AM, the former WDOK-AM, in late 1965.) I had a couple of guys over the years who came pretty close. John Larsch was a kid when I hired him. They called him the "fastest talking disc jockey" and I renamed him Jackson Armstrong. Don't forget the "Wild Child". Dick Kemp. When he cracked that mic he took off at a hundred miles an hour. Funny, too! They jumped out of the speakers at you, both of them. Even so, Myers and Mad Daddy were one of a kind...or should I say two of a kind?"

The late Carl Reese was another of Myers' "Cleveland contemporaries". In a conversation at the Rock and Roll Hall of Fame for the debut of the book <u>1950s Radio in Color</u>, (Kent State University Press, 2011) he remembered Myers with a fond smile that only added to his mystique. Reese recalled, "I was on a different station when he was doing that Daddy thing. Sometimes I'd listen to him on WHK on my way to work. Crazy show! I met him a few times and was surprised how different he was off the air. Nice enough guy. Smart. Quiet, and he just smiled a lot and nodded his head. I couldn't tell you what we talked about. What do you call it? Small talk. Everybody knew everybody back then. We would have recognized each other if we passed on the street, maybe stopped to say hello, but I can't say I really knew Myers. I don't really know anyone who did."

Reese added a different perspective on Myers as Mad Daddy. "I got to WHK a few years after he left, but there were people who remembered working with him. People talk about him today, and I'm not sure exactly why. Don't get me wrong. Talented guy, but it was different then. Maybe it was his time slot. I'm not sure he would have had an audience at any other time. I came to 'HK after he was gone. Remember "Your Captain of the Morning"? The show I did in the early sixties was for that kind of audience. Like when I did nights at WERE a few years before. You didn't want to shock or scare anyone. Myers was pretty loud. Middle of the day? You had housewives listening. Plus, he was playing songs by "colored" musicians. You didn't hear that on the big shows. Then the dinner hour. Families had the radio on at supper time for background. That wasn't a show to eat to."

Reese added, "Look at the competition during the day. Bill Gordon, Tommy Edwards, (Phil) McLean. Bill Randle was a superstar...", and with a sly grin added, "...and he reminded you of that constantly!" (Author's note: Randle was notorious for his huge ego, but even his detractors had to admit he could back up every word of it.) "Where did they put him? Evenings. When mom and dad were watching TV and the kids were in garages, driving around in cars or listening in bed with the sound turned down low. Myers was on at the right time, but maybe the only time for it to work."

You can argue that Pete Myers failed to reach the full potential of his alter-ego Mad Daddy, but he wasn't alone. Radio programmers demanded a new type of personality to bring in the audience, and Myers delivered that personality beyond their expectations. The programmers weren't prepared for this radical departure and failed to market and exploit the Mad Daddy character to its fullest potential. If Pete Myers had stayed in Northeast Ohio, his Mad Daddy may well have become one of the most respected and revered voices in local radio. Instead, he accepted a small role in the world's biggest radio market of New York City, and was sadly destined to become a footnote in broadcasting history.

Chapter Ten

Promotion....or Bribery?

Legacy can be difficult to define, and all three of these key players… Freed, Mintz and Myers… can rightfully claim their place in the history of popular music, though much of it can be based on legend and that heavily favors Alan Freed. All played a crucial role in the way rock and roll was eventually accepted and grew within our culture. All used their own unique talents to further their careers and the culture, but two met tragic ends. Let's review who won, who lost and how.

Freed's story is well documented. He played the radio game of that time riding to fame and fortune, but along the way stepped over a line in the sand challenging racism and his past dealings came back to take him down. Remember the post war attitudes toward race. Freed demanded the audience restrictions at a May 1958 Boston concert be taken down and that request was refused. He's quoted as telling the audience, "It looks like the Boston police don't want you to have a good time" and that was all the authorities needed to hear suggesting Freed was inciting a riot. The show was stopped, Freed was taken away and the gauntlet was thrown. Freedom was a subjective term to many back then defined by racial discrimination and while Freed couldn't face charges for fighting racism, his actions did give the incentive to certain parties to look for ways to silence him and they rose to the challenge.

WINS didn't need controversy and Freed was released from his contract claiming the station failed to "stand behind my policies and principles", but that was only the beginning. At the time disc jockeys held great power over what they played on the air. Music publishers and artists accepted this as part of the game. Freed's still had name recognition with a big radio career, movies, a TV show and plenty of press to back him up. New York's WABC brought him on board in

June 1958 to make the most of his notoriety…but there would be a major stumbling block.

Disc jockeys could argue that the music they aired was an extension of their personality and what made their shows unique. It could also add greatly to their bank accounts if an artist, record label or publisher was willing to "play the game", and that game was payola. It was basically "pay to play". Money or even writing credits would be transferred to a personality in return for airing a song. It resulted in some artists selling records based on exposure rather than talent. Some in the business simply wrote it off as promotion, while others called it bribery. He certainly wasn't alone, but Alan Freed knew that game well.

"Pay to play", payola, was the way many labels worked and, apparently, very successfully for many years. It was more unethical than illegal under close scrutiny but wasn't discussed publicly because it essentially said that money rather than the public's reaction or even the artist's talent determined a song or an act's longevity. It could also be extremely profitable if a jock was willing to cooperate. Still, that practice wasn't getting favorable press and it threw a long shadow on some of radio's biggest personalities and stations. WNEW tried to head off the bad press by hosting an on-air panel discussion with four of its most recognized jocks including Pete Myers, William B. Williams, Gene Klavan and Dee Finch. The station's general manager John Sullivan and PD Mark Olds were there as well as was *Billboard*'s Paul Ackerman and the *Journal-American*'s radio editor Altra Baer. The show was moderated by WNEW's news director Martin Weldon so it was pretty much the station putting itself under a magnifying glass. It wasn't likely the radio staff would give the press an opportunity for even greater scrutiny, and the management didn't want any surprises, but the questioning was surprisingly frank as were some of the responses.

With all agreeing beforehand that payola did indeed exist and was a widespread practice, the central theme was a question, "Have you been approached with a payola offer?". Keeping in mind that word "approached" is far different than "accepted", both Myers and Williams openly admitted they had. Oddly enough, Myers may have raised some eyebrows when he replied," Well, I've been approached but I've always turned it down, because - well, maybe I'm afraid of being caught. Probably that's it. I guess I'm as honest as any jockey." The issue that might have been lost on Myers and was being sensationalized in the press is that a lot of disc jockeys simply weren't portrayed as honest. Williams backed up Myers saying that he was never offered cash, but color TVs were very expensive back then and a label offered him a set if he would "lean" on a certain record, which he rejected. As Williams put it, "I wish I knew psychologically why I turned it down. I think part of it is something that Pete touched on – pride in the fact that I would then not have control over my show." The panelists all admitted that an occasional lunch or even Christmas gift was acceptable within limits, stressing there was a difference between a thank you and a bribe, but Williams also frankly admitted knowing a network jock who kept a weeklong daily schedule of meals and meetings with label reps., though not saying he accepted the offers. That would have likely had the feds knocking on his door demanding names.

Klavan suggested the parties offering payola, not only to disc jockeys but also the press, should be looked at as well, and Ackerman brought up that records themselves could be a form of bribery. Hundreds of promotional records could be forwarded to jocks or stations that would later be distributed to stores for sale. He pointed out that this practice likely violated copyright and publishing fees because songwriters weren't paid for promotional giveaways. The panel also agreed that the elephant in the room was the Internal Revenue Service. The legitimacy of payola promotion was iffy. Not declaring it on your taxes was not, which was essentially how Alan Freed was brought down.

Myers echoed Klavan's call that promoters be investigated, adding that artist livelihoods were affected because payola was "siphoning off of this money in front of the artists' anticipated royalties. He doesn't get anything until this whole thing is washed out." All agreed that payola was a "dark cloud" and called for further investigation beyond interaction with just the disc jockeys who were in the cross hairs. As Myers pointed out, some of the effects of payola were plainly evident, especially when a song was added at key stations as a tool in promoting it to other radio outlets. He stated, "I think that when a record suddenly jumps in the first two days into a position of 32 or 29 or 19 on one of these lists, and is then mailed back to the music publisher in New York so he can take it around elsewhere and show that the song has gained commercial acceptance in another market, this boosts its acceptance in market after market and starts the chain reaction that can build a hit in radio, and payola often comes into play here".

GM Sullivan emphasized that WNEW would do all it could to battle payola, claiming he "didn't have any great deal of knowledge of payola." He did say, "I do have some knowledge of WNEW and, to my knowledge, it doesn't happen here." Not suggesting that Sullivan was being dishonest in any way, but the key words he mentioned were "to my knowledge". He did have the backs of his air staff saying if he did hear about a jock taking a bribe, "I'm sure that I would probably faint because, honestly it would be a foreign or alien realization for me….I know how much money (the jocks) make, and as long as they're worth it, they'll be here unless they begin to augment it from someplace else".

Two takeaways from the panel that evening. Ratings determined if a jock in the most competitive radio market in the world was worth it, and then…as now… audience could be fickle. Some might rationalize that you make as much money as you can while you can, even if you dipped your toes into potentially dangerous waters. The second? Organized crime. Mob influence was very evident on a number of levels in 1950s New York and the recording industry was no different. You would have stepped into a minefield if you broached that subject, especially to one of the city's biggest radio audiences.

The radio industry was overseen by the Federal Communications Commission and the writing was on the wall. If a station was denied a broadcast license or its renewal, that station was out of business. Payola wasn't exactly illegal in 1959, but it did carry some risk especially regarding bad publicity. Plenty of jocks were willing to take that risk, but time was running out. That November, Arkansas Congressman Oren Harris, a former federal judge, led a subcommittee investigating the influence of payola on commercial music and a lot of influential people in the music industry scrambled to cover their butts. The American Authors and Composers Guild admitted that form of ...let's call it "promotion" ...was a "prime factor in selecting music for broadcasts and that the Federal Communications Commission and the Federal Trade Commission know of this but have failed to act upon it", though the National Disc Jockeys Council issued a strong denial.

A lot of big names were at risk as were their employers. Dick Clark was a major player, and *American Bandstand* was a TV brand that carried a lot of influence. On November 17th, the ABC-TV network demanded and got a commitment from Clark that he "never received any personal considerations" to promote certain artists or records. Just to cover all the bases, the network also demanded Clark and some other key personnel to drop any financial interests they may have with music publishing houses and other fields. Clark agreed, but the producer for *American Bandstand* opted to resign. Days later, WABC demanded Freed follow suit and sign a statement did not get compensation from outside parties to promote certain artists or records.

Uh-oh.

It seems that Alan Freed heavily promoted certain records by the Flamingoes, the Moonglows and especially Chuck Berry's "Maybelline" ...all that carried the Freed name as a co-writer! The conflict of interest seemed apparent, though Freed claimed it wasn't payola, refused to sign the statement calling it "an insult to me reputation and integrity", and soon found himself without a job.

WABC reported Freed's dismissal with a terse statement that simply read. "This afternoon radio station WABC exercised its contractual right to terminate its agreement with Alan Freed". His firing made the front page of his old hometown paper, the *Plain Dealer*, and to add insult to injury, it misspelled his name as "Allen". On the TV side, WNEW's general manager Bennet H. Korn announced that in light of recent events he was meeting with Freed to "discuss the background and future of the show", promising "I'm going to find out what's going on". Freed vowed, "I'm a fighter and I'll fight", but as it turned out later that week Freed was also let go from his TV duties by mutual consent even though he did reportedly sign a document stating there were no improprieties on his part. To be perfectly fair, one part of that dispute stemmed from an objection by the American Federation of Television and Radio Artists (AFTRA) claiming many of the musical guests were not paid when they lip synched their records, which Freed said was standard practice and turns out it would be for years to come. The house of cards would fall within hours.

The American Society for Composers, Authors and Publishers (ASCAP) took a hard stand that it was against payola but once again admitted it was a problem. Alan Freed and his financial records were subpoenaed, and it wasn't long before, as TV's Ricky Ricardo would say, he had some "splainin'" to do. It was in black and white. Yes, Freed did get checks from record companies, but he said they were consulting fees, not payola.

The public wasn't going to buy it. Keep in mind that the quiz scandal was still fresh in people's minds and this sort of chicanery sold newspapers. This wasn't going to be ignored. By November 30th, Freed was quoted as saying, "My career has gone down the drain". Sadly, that statement would prove to be true, and his problems were far from over.

In 1960, a Congressional amendment to the Federal Communications Act outlawed "under-the-table payments and require broadcasters to disclose if airplay for a song has been purchased." Freed wasn't the only jock to get busted. There were $50 a week DJ's who took in tens of thousands of dollars for similar deals and that came to an abrupt halt. Dick Clark cooperated and presented himself well to the committee leading to a long and illustrious career. Freed was abrasive and defiant. He didn't do himself any favors.

Over the next few years, he would be indicted by a federal grand jury for tax evasion linked to the payola payments and was handed a bill for nearly $38,000 he owed the government. It was a debt that he could never repay. Add to that the dark cloud over his name from the negative publicity and it wasn't likely he would find work with a station of any real status. He headed to Santa Monica, California, where he took a job at KDAY-AM that lasted a couple of years before he left when the station wouldn't allow him to promote his stage shows. His next stop was WQAM / Miami, a job that would only last two months, possibly the result of Freed's drinking. By 1964 he was back on the West Coast on KNOB / Long Beach, an FM station in an era when AM was still king. In January 1965, at just 43 years old, Freed lost his battle with uremia and cirrhosis spurred on by his alcoholism.

Freed's death made front page headlines…" below the fold" as they say…in his old hometown newspaper, the *Cleveland Plain Dealer*. Of course, it mentioned his meteoric rise, the Moondog Ball, his days in New York, and the payola scandal claiming Freed was accused of accepting more than $30,000 from seven record companies. The paper pointed out that Freed finally admitted to accepting $2700, paid a $300 fine and was indicted by a federal grand jury in March 1964 on charges of income tax evasion, much of it based on the payola money, to the tune of $37,000. Not the postscript one would hope for in what many now recognize as a groundbreaking career.

His remains were originally interred in Hartsdale, New York, but starting in 2002 his ashes were on display at Cleveland's Rock and Roll Hall of Fame. They remained there until 2014 when the family transferred the urn to a grave at Cleveland's Lake View Cemetery, the final home of President James Garfield, former Untouchable Eliot Ness and many other notable names. In a ceremony headed up by E Street band guitarist and media mogul "Little Steven" Van Zandt, Freed was memorialized under a juke box sized gravestone that bore his image. It begs the question. Like Pete "Mad Daddy" Myers, should Alan Freed have stayed and capitalized on his success in Cleveland? It's not likely the music industry and popular culture would have evolved at the same pace, but Freed paid the price. His role in the history of popular music was assured, maybe not at that particular time on a national level, but Freed might have even lived to see the museum he helped name.

Let's also look at Pete Myers. This begs the obvious question: With the rise of the disc jockey in the 1950s and 60s, why was Daddy different? A number of reasons. There's one we call "the forbidden fruit". The sense of teenage rebellion is a powerful force, and if your parents say for example "Don't drink water!", a typical kid is heading for the tap to see why not. That was one of the cornerstones of early rock and roll. Black music appealing to white kids in, let's call it what it was, a racist post war America seems like the devil your son or daughter was listening to under their pillow. That went for the people bringing them the music, too. Mad Daddy was so over the top with his colorful language and "race records" that parents got nervous. Plus, his short-lived TV series with the actual sight of Myers as Mad Daddy and the news coverage following the jump in Lake Erie didn't endear him to the older crowd, but it sure appealed to his target audience.

Here's another point to consider. When the Mad Daddy hit the airwaves, commercial radio had been around for more than a generation. It was so deeply entrenched into American culture that television had a hard time overcoming its popularity. There are a number of reasons for that. TVs were very expensive when they first hit the market, and there wasn't a whole lot of programming. There might be just a few hours a day, and then the so-called test pattern to fine tune the picture. However, there's another critical point and that was simply imagination. Some media consumers were hesitant to switch over to TV because "radio had better pictures". The TV imagery was never as vivid as the way they envisioned radio performers. When you consider this, you can imagine how the radio audience may have thought Mad Daddy looked when they heard his maniacal laugh, machine gun delivery and in studio sound effects. Plus, his live appearances helped sell that image. His pink Pontiac, the swirling hooded cape and ghoulish grin drew attention both good and bad. Good for the young audience that saw the image they likely expected, and bad for the horrified older generation that saw the same thing. As superficial as it truly is even today, image is a critical component to success on TV. Dick Clark had matinee looks and appealed to a national audience. Not so with Freed and Myers, but to Cleveland's credit, the young audience was able to see beyond that for the entertainment content they offered.

Let's also take another look at the birth of the "generation gap" that would bloom into outright rebellion a decade later. Post war America in the 1940s and 50s produced a separate teenage culture, and we can put some of the blame on TV which drew an older audience desperate for escape. As TVs made their way into more homes it kept folks away from theaters and clubs and we also saw the birth of the "couch potato". The energy and excitement of being a teenager wasn't being shown on TV, and for a generation that now had its own fashions, spare cash, cars and music the Mad Daddy was the standard bearer for a demographic rediscovering the new form of radio. The difference in lifestyle was now being reflected to a great degree on transistor radios and car tuners and was far more accessible.

Another possible lure was the fact that Mad Daddy, for lack of a better term, was a sort of "audio cartoon character". It was an alter ego, as if two people occupied the same body and came out at the appropriate times. Was Daddy's delivery that much different than jocks around the country? There's no question that he was unique, but let's explore that a bit. You had "howlers, yowlers and screamers" on stations around the country, though Mad Daddy took it to a different level. You had jocks like Maurice "Hot Rod" Hulbert, "Jocko" Henderson and Hal Jackson all who had distinctive on-air patter and were heard by audiences in New York and other markets, and even smaller markets like Columbus, Ohio, had Hoyte "Dr. Bop" Locke and Eddie Saunders. It was like that around the country but again, in…let's call it what it was…racist post WWII America, they played the same music Freed and Myers aired, to primarily urban audiences. Leo Mintz saw the crossover audience and was able to successfully cross promote with the help of the Moondog and Mad Daddy.

Yet another point to consider is how parents perceived these new entertainers, disc jockeys. Once again, we take a stand that the payola scandal of the 1950s wasn't really about tax evasion, though it was the legal avenue that brought plenty of jocks down. It may well have centered on race. Alan Freed pioneered a new sound on radio, but he was only an average looking guy. His views on music and racial equality were far from average. On the other hand, as online columnist and educator Matthew Lasar points out in his Radio Survivor blog, Dick Clark…the Philadelphia jock who later hosted *American Bandstand* and was able to escape the worst of the payola scandal… was a young, handsome, TV friendly face who didn't seem a threat even though he took a bold step during the civil rights era. Quoting Clark's *New York Times* obituary, Lasar mentioned the *Dick Clark Show* in Atlanta had a mixed audience of teenagers in the audience. Clark also demanded racial barriers be eliminated on *American Bandstand* in 1956 since much of the music came from black entertainers. This was an especially gutsy move by Clark because that same year *The Nat King Cole Show* became the first network variety show to be hosted by a black entertainer. Great entertainment, huge audience, but one major problem. No national sponsor leading to the show's demise the following year. Clark didn't look "dangerous" even though he was taking giant steps toward integrating TV. Myers' Mad Daddy played down and dirty R & B. With his imagery could he have possibly survived hosting a musically based TV show, especially with the artists he played? You could see your daughter going out with Dick Clark. Daddy was a different story. Much could be said about Freed in that same vein, though he did have a TV show focused heavily on music rather than image. Still, he never had the TV success of Dick Clark.

Dick Clark's name lives on long after his death, much of it linked to his TV work. Along with extensive historical research focused in his life and career Alan Freed's name is immortalized in songs from artists ranging from the Animals and Neil Diamond to the Ramones and Marc Bolan's T.Rex, all Rock and Roll Hall of Fame inductees. Myers was commemorated by Lux Interior and the Cramps in their song "Mad Daddy".

But what about the guy who influenced their shows and helped guide their careers?

Sadly, like Freed and Myers, Leo Mintz died young. He was just 65 when he was claimed by cancer in early November 1976, having seen his Record Rendezvous stores grow to five successful locations though eventually falling victim to online commerce and the end of the shopping mall era. Mintz wasn't a musician; he was a marketer and a savvy one at that. He may or may not have seen the long-term impact of crossover music from urban to white audiences on popular culture, but he certainly saw the immediate demand in those early days and knew how to deliver product to the masses. Mintz earned a life he enjoyed with grandchildren, golf and the occasional nip of Scotch. He was well loved by family and many friends, and on the day of his funeral his young grandson was struck by the long procession of cars making their way to his final resting place at Solon, Ohio's, Mount Olive Cemetery. Mintz has some well-deserved recognition from the Rock and Roll Hall of Fame, almost assuredly deserves more, and is also prominently recognized in a highly regarded New York musical titled *Rock and Roll Man*. It focuses on Freed but honors Mintz' influence even recreating his

Prospect Avenue store for the play. He was laid to rest with a bottle and putter in his casket, a reminder of a truly remarkable and influential life and career.

In 2023, the former record store on Prospect sat abandoned. There was no plaque marking its significance, yet along with the Hall of Fame on the shores of Lake Erie and its archives on Woodland Avenue, it stands as a monument to three unique personalities... Mintz, the Moondog and the Mad Daddy... and the role they played in shaping popular culture worldwide.

Bibliography

III, A. I. (2021, January 27). *Rebels of the Golden age: The style icons of the '50s*. Mantle Magazine. https://www.mantlemagazine.com/index. php/2019/04/19/re bels-of-the-golden-age/.

15 Injured, Boston Bans Rock 'n' Roll. (1958, May 5). *Akron Beacon Journal.*, p. 20.

ABC Network Official Denies Charge Made by Ex-Disc Jockey Alan Freed. (1960, May 3). *Coshocton Tribune.*, p. 1.

Action Line. (1966, December 29). *Akron Beacon Journal.*, p. 1.

Alan Freed chronological history in newsprint. (n.d.). https://www. vocalgroupharmony.com/ALANFREED/AlanFreed50.htm

Alan Freed Files Bankruptcy Plea. (1951, May 9). *Akron Beacon Journal.*

Alan Freed Pleads Innocent in Payola. (1960, May 20). *Akron Beacon Journal.*, p. 53.and, Seven Others F

Alan Freed to Enter New York Radio Work. (1954, August 5). *Salem News.*

Alan Freed's Video Show May Expand. (1950a, April 24). *Salem News.*

Allen Freed is 'Fired' in Payola Tiff. (1959, November 22). *Cleveland Plain Dealer*, pp. 1–14.

Anderson, Stan. (December 14, 1949.) Third TV Station, WXEL, Opens This Saturday. *Cleveland Press*. P. 29034.

Anderson, Stanley. (November 14, 1947.) WEWS in Cleveland. *Cleveland Press*. p.39

Barclay , M. (2016, November 29). *The Weird and True Story of Moondog*. Macleans.ca. https://macleans.ca/culture/the-weird-and-true-story-of-moondog/

Batz., B. (1987, June 7). Leo Mintz Shortchanged for Coining Phrase. *Dayton Daily News & Journal Herald. The Magazine.*, p. 8.

Bernard, Bruce. (Ed.) (1999.) *Century*. London: Phaidron Press Limited.

Better Watch Out. (April 12, 1958.) *Cleveland Press.*

"Blore is Winner of Gavin Award." (1962, January 13). *Billboard*, 6.

Boston, New Haven Prohibit Rock 'n' Roll Music Shows. (1958, May 6). *Cleveland Plain Dealer*, p. 28.

Bundy, J. (1958, June 2). "Deejay Competition Booms Stunts, Contests, Gimmicks." *The Billboard*, 70(21), 4.

Bundy, J. (1960, August 29). Vox Jox. *The Billboard*, 22.

Bundy, J. (1960, November 21). Vox Jox. *The Billboard*.

Bundy, J. (1961, November 20). "Comedy LP Laughs Gain on Nation's Air." *Billboard*, 13–19.

Bundy, J. (1961, May 29). "D,J,s Test Traffic Scene in 3-Station Promotions." *Billboard*, 73(21), 16.

Bundy, J. (1961, September 25). Vox Jox. *Billboard*, 15.

Bundy, J. (1962, April 29). Vox Jox. *Billboard*, 32.

Bundy, J. (1962, August 25). Vox Jox. *Billboard*, 26.

Bundy, J. (1962, October 20). Vox Jox. *Billboard*, 74(42), 27.

Bundy, J. (1962, November 17). Vox Jox. *Billboard*, 74(16), 36.

Calta, Louis. "Pete Myers, 40, of WNEW is Dead*." New York Times*. October 5, 1968.

Canton Has Alan Freed. (1958, April 6). *Akron Beacon Journal.*, pp. 10-C.

Cleveland Dance Fails from Too Much Success. (1952, March 22). *Salem News*.

Cleveland's Pioneer Station Treks Across Half a Century - This is a golden radio year for WHK. (January 1, 1971.) *Plain Dealer.*

Cash Box. Pic of the week—Virgil Brinnon (WJW-Cleveland, Ohio) . (1955). Photograph, New York.

Condon, G. E. (1954, September 23). On the Air – Barry Nelson's Double Life is Split...Johnny (Always Hustling) Andrews...Tom Fields' Jinx. *Cleveland Plain Dealer*, p. 17.

Condon, G. E. (1954, January 7). On the air - "King of the Moondogs" Quits WJW to Sign with New York Station. *Cleveland Plain Dealer*, p. 30.

Condon, G. (1958, May 12). 'Mad Daddy' to Switch. *Cleveland Plain Dealer.*, p. 29.

Condon, G. E. (1953, May 29). On the air - "Moondoggers" king' back on the job after narrow escape from death. *Cleveland Plain Dealer*, p. 6.

Condon., G. E. (1958, December 28). Condon on '58 - TV Radio Realm Was a Busy Place. *Cleveland Plain Dealer*, pp. 8-C.

Condon, G. E. (1956b, March 21). On the Air - Research Bureau Reports Two Western Films Most Popular Here. *Cleveland Plain Dealer*, p. 16.

Condon., G. E. (1958, June 21). Condon on the Hour - It's Time to Tell How Clock Gave DJ the Works. *Cleveland Plain Dealer*, p. 16.

Condon., G. (1958, May 16). Condon on Miscellany - Danny Thomas Has June Cleveland Date; 'Mad Daddy' is Off for The Months. *Cleveland Plain Dealer.*, p. 11.

Condon., G. (1958, June 13). Condon on Potpourri - More Staff Changes Are Seen as WHK Drops NBC Network July 31. *Cleveland Plain Dealer.*, p. 19.

Condon., G. (1958, May 12). Mad Daddy to Switch. *Cleveland Plain Dealer.*, p. 29.

Cullison., A. (1950, March 12). Disc Jocks Move Into Niteries. *Akron Beacon Journal.*

Cullison., A. (1958, January 17). Giveaways Slipping - Isolation Booths May Go Begging. *Akron Beacon Journal.*, p. 20.

Cullison., A. (1956, December 19). Teenagers May Like It. *Akron Beacon Journal.*, p. 30.

Daddy Hurts Mommy. (1959, May 2). *Cleveland Plain Dealer.*, p. 18.

'Daddy Syndicating'. (1959, June 13). *Cleveland Plain Dealer.*, p. 21.

"Deejay Starr Exits WNEW." (1960, April 4). *The Billboard*, 9.

DeLuca, David. (September, 1984.) The Mad, Mad Daddy of Cleveland Radio. *Cleveland Magazine.* pp. 82-85 & 151-153.

Disc Jock Moves Into Nitery. (1951, March 12). *Akron Beacon Journal.*

Disk Jockey Has Experts Helping on Chute Jump. (1958, June 13). *Cleveland Plain Dealer.*, p. 19.

DJ Alan Freed Loses TV, Radio Jobs in Gotham. (1959, November 24). *News-Messenger.*, p. 1.

"D.J. Myers to WNEW." (1959, June 15). *The Billboard*, 7.

"DJ 'Half Price Pick' Tie Up". (1958, November 24). *The Billboard*, 70(47), 3.

"DJA Meet to Finalize Pre-Convention Plans." (1959, November 2). *The Billboard*, 4.

Dramarama Productions (Producer.) & Paul Eichgrom (Writer/Producer/ Director.)

 (1998.) Rock and Roll Invaders: The AM Radio Deejays. (Available from Berklee

College of Music - Stan Getz Library1140 Boylston St., Boston, MA 02215

Elliot, Bob & Goulding, Ray. (1975.) *Write If You Get Work: The Best of Bob and Ray.* New York: Random House.

Ensminger, D. A. (2011). *Visua Vitriol: The Street Art and Subcultures of the Punk and Hardcore Generation.* Univ. Press of Mississippi.

Faggen, G. (1964, November 7). Vox Jox. *Billboard*, 76(45), 26.

Faggen, G. (1965, March 13). "Landers Exits WNEW; Tate his Replacer." *Billboard*, 77(11), 72.

Faggen, G. (1965, March 27). "There's No Place like WNEW Business." *Billboard*, 77(13), 48.

Faggen, G. (1965, January 16). Vox Jox. *Billboard*, 77(3), 39.

Feran, Tom. & Heldenfels, R.D. (1997.) *Ghoulardi – Inside Cleveland TV's Wildest Ride*. Cleveland: Gray & Company.

Feran, Tom. (June 17, 2003.) The meteoric rise of Mad Daddy. *Plain Dealer.* pp. E1-E3

Flanagan., J. B. (1964, June 5). Root High Graduate Aims High in Radio. *Plain Dealer.*, p. 8.

Former DJ Here Takes Own Life. (October 5, 1968.) *Cleveland Plain Dealer.* p. 52

Frankel, Jim. (July 8, 1958.) Mello Jellocast. *Cleveland Press.* p. 20

Frankel, Jim. (June 1, 1959.) Pete (Madaddy) Meyers Moving to New York Station. *Cleveland Press.* p. 22

Freed Case Ruling Stands. (1951c, March 22). *Akron Beacon Journal.*

Freed Has Show. (1950, April 8). *Salem News.*

Freed Plans Appeal on Court's Ruling. (1950a, February 28). *Salem News.*

Freed Says He Sought to 'Work for Himself'. (1950, February 21). *Akron Beacon Journal.*, p. 38.

Freed Says Rock Music Good, Williams Labels It Garbage. (1958, August 13). *Akron Beacon Journal.*

Fong-Torres, Ben. (1998). *The Hits Just Keep On Coming: The History of Top 40 Radio.* San Francisco: Miller-Freeman Books.

Gallagher, Nancy. (July 30, 1958.) Edwards Cuts Disc on Boy-Girl Theme. *Cleveland Press.* p. 28

Garner, D. (2015). *'Sam Phillips: The Man Who Invented Rock 'n' Roll,' by Peter Guralnick.* New York Times This Morning.

Gavin, B. (1963, January 12). Programming Newsletter. *Blllboard,* 75(2), 37.

Gavin, B. (1963, January 12). Programming Newsletter. *Billboard,* 75(2), 34.

Gillespie, Rev. L. (1954, June 27). Community Relations - Letter About the Moon Dog ...Question of Racial Sensitiveness...Radio and TV Censorshiip. *Cleveland Plain Dealer,* p. 34.

Glascock, H. L. (1967, April 8). "There's Only One." *Billboard ,* 32–38.

Godfrey. Donald G. (2006.) *Methods of historical analysis in electronic media.* Mahwah, New Jersey: Lawrence Erlebaum Associates, Inc.

Grevatt, R. (1961, November 20). "Selling Comics like Singles Pays Off." *Billboard,* 19.

Hall, C. (1970, August 22). Vox Jox. *Billboard,* 82(34), 54.

Halloween Pranks Get Station Break. (1958, October 25). *Cleveland Plain Dealer.,* p. 22.

Halper, Donna. (1994.) Halper's History of Radio. Retrieved February 20, 2007 from http://www.old-time.com/halper/halper37.html

Hearing on Alan Freed Ban Set for Tuesday. (1950, February 17). *Akron Beacon Journal.,* p. 1.

Henahan., D. (1957, June 23). Is It Music or Garbage? *Akron Beacon Journal.,* pp. 1 D.

Herschman., I. (1985, October 24). Rock and Roll Hall of Fame in Cleveland Makes Sense. *Dayton Daily News.,* p. 14.

Hilliard, Robert L. & Keith, Michael C. (1997). *The Broadcast Century: A Biography of American Broadcasting.* Newton, Massachusetts: Butterworth-Heinemann.

Hinckley, David. (April 7, 2005.) Man out of Time - Mad Daddy. *New York Daily News.*

Holliday, Johnny. & Moore, Stephen. (2002). *Johnny Holliday: from Rock to Jock.* Champaign, Illinois: Sports Publishing L.L.C.

Hunt, Jay. (2005.) Radio Broadcasting History, Radio People (Pete Myers aka Mad Daddy.) Retrieved March 17, 2008 from http://www.440. com/_pmyers.html

Hurd, Christine. (March 18, 2016.) Ernie Myers, veteran radio broadcaster, 86. *San Diego Union Tribune.*

Infoplease. 1958. Retrieved February 19, 2007 from http://www.infoplease. com/year/1958.html#us

Jackson, John A. (1991.) *Big Beat Heat: Alan Freed and the Early Years of Rock and Roll.* New York: Schirmer Books.

"Jocks Shift; Collins, Lowe to New Jobs." (1959, July 20). *The Billboard,* 7.

Kane., R. W. (1962, June 13). Channel Checker - Neal's Show Moves Along with Indians. *Plain Dealer.*, p. 33.

Kane., R. W. (1958, March 22). Channel Swimmer - Some Wavy Gravy from 'Mad Daddy'. . *Cleveland Plain Dealer.*, p. 20.

Kane., R. (1959, January 3). Channel Swimmer - Why Do Radio Hams Always Talk in Jargon? *Cleveland Plain Dealer.*, p. 17.

Keith, Michael C. (2000.) *The Radio Station.* Woburn, MA: Focal Press.

Kleiner., D. (1957, April 12). Alan Freed Discovers Bach-Und-Roll. *Salem News.*, p. 10.

Knows-It-All: Pete "Mad Daddy" Myers. Retrieved September 19, 2006 from http://www.homestayfinder.com/Dictionary.aspx?q=WKNR

"KYA Plays List Flexible Way." (1967, July 29). *Billboard,* 28.

Little Character. (December 20, 1958.) *Cleveland Press – Home Magazine.* p. 21

Mad Daddy. (July 16, 1958.) *Cleveland Press.* p. 29

Mad Daddy Tries It in New York – Briefly. (July 14, 1959.) *Cleveland Press.* p. 19

Mad Daddy Turned Off for 90 Days. (May, 1958.) Retrieved March 4, 2008 from http://www.freewebs.com/maddaddy/Mad DaddyOffAir. jpg

McCormack, John. (October 29, 1948.) Lend Eye, Too, New Station Asks of City's Radio Fans. *Cleveland News.*

"McIntyre Steers WCAR to Top 40." (1971, August 14). *Billboard, 83*(33), 23.

McLellan, Dennis. (December 2, 2008.) Bill Drake dies at 71; 'Boss Radio' inventor spread less-talk format across country. *Los Angeles Times.*

McMahon, Ed. & Fisher, David. (2007.) *When Television* Was *Young: The Inside Story with Memories by Legends of the Small Screen.* Nashville, Tenn: Thomas Nelson.

Mellow, Jan. (July 14, 1958.) 'Mad Daddy' Bails Out Into Bale of Publicity, *Cleveland News.* p. 23

"Miss Crane Tokyo Bride". (1950, December 28.) *New York Times.* P. 2.

Mitchell., G. (1958, May 13). Alan Freed Resigns After Riot. *Dayton Daily News.*, p. 33.

Mitchell., G. (1958, April 14). Idea May Spread - Alan Freed Teen Club to Get Miami Tryout. *Dayton Daily News.*, p. 16.

Moerer, Craig. (Date Unknown.) "Pete Myers - DJ 'Mad Daddy.' Retrieved February 20, 2007 from http://www.recordsbymail.com/madDaddy.php.

"'Moondog' Alan Freed Dead at 43". (1965, January 21). *Cleveland Plain Dealer.* P.1-9

Moondog Ball is Halted as 6000 Crash Arena Gate. (1952, March 22). *Cleveland Plain Dealer*, p. 1.

The "Moondogger" covers lots of ground. (1953, November 22). *Cleveland Plain Dealer*, pp. 52-D.

"More Mad Daddy". (1958, March 29). *Cleveland Plain Dealer.* P. 24.

"Murray the K to Exit WINS." (1965, February 6). *Billboard*, 46.

Myers, Pete. (1958). Greasy Dedications (Recorded by Pete Myers.) On *The Mad Daddy Wavy Gravy.* (CD). New York, N.Y: Norton Records. (2003)

Myers, Pete. (1959). Hanging from the Ceiling. (Recorded by Pete Myers.) On *The Mad Daddy Wavy Gravy.* (CD). New York, N.Y: Norton Records. (2003)

Myers, Pete. (1959). Mad Daddy Batty Bucks. (Recorded by Pete Myers.) On *The Mad Daddy Wavy Gravy*. (CD). New York, N.Y: Norton Records. (2003)

Myers, Pete. (1959). I Love a Practical Joke. (Recorded by Pete Myers.) On *The Mad Daddy Wavy Gravy*. (CD). New York, N.Y: Norton Records. (2003)

Myers, Pete. (1959). Round Sounds. (Recorded by Pete Myers.) On *The Mad Daddy Wavy Gravy*. (CD). New York, N.Y: Norton Records. (2003)

Myers, Pete. (1959). The Winky Eye Goes Out (Recorded by Pete Myers.) On *The Mad Daddy Wavy Gravy*. (CD). New York, N.Y: Norton Records. (2003)

Myers, Pete. (1958). Wavy Gravy Flow (Recorded by Pete Myers.) On *The Mad Daddy Wavy Gravy*. (CD). New York, N.Y: Norton Records. (2003)

Myers, Pete. (1958). What is a Fisteris? (Recorded by Pete Myers.) On *The Mad Daddy Wavy Gravy*. (CD). New York, N.Y: Norton Records. (2003)

Myers, Pete. (1959). Zoomeratin' Alphabet (Recorded by Pete Myers.) On *The Mad Daddy Wavy Gravy*. (CD). New York, N.Y: Norton Records. (2003)

New History Play on Broadway. (1948, January 24). *Akron Beacon Journal*. p. 7.

New Scoring System for Arena Races. (1959, February 9). *Cleveland Plain Dealer.*, p. 31.

New York's WINS Adds Top Cleveland Deejay. (February 8, 1964.) *Billboard*. p. 12

Nichols, K. (1978, January 26). Movie on Disc Jockey Freed Should Pain True Akron Fans. *Akron Beacon Journal*. D-18.

Nichols,, K. (1963, January 21). Alan Freed, Rock 'n' Roll .Pied Piper', Dies at 43. *Akron Beacon Journal.*, pp. B-10.

No Condition is Permanent: Pete 'Mad Daddy' Myers Retrieved September 22, 2008 from permanentcondition.blogspot.com/2007/10/pete-mad-daddy-myers-final-whk_9762.html - 32k

N.Y. Radio Station Drops Alan Freed. (1959, November 22). *Dayton Daily News.*, p. 8.

O'Connell, T. (1954, September 11). Alan Freed, WJW Battle Over Moon Dog Rights. *Cleveland Plain Dealer*, p. 16.

O'Connell, T. (1954, May 1). Alan Freed Hosts Moondog Affair Tonight in Newark. *Cleveland Plain Dealer*, p. 23.

O'Connor, Clint. (July 10, 2004.) DJ legend Bill Randle dead at 81. *Plain Dealer*. p. A1

Offineer, B. (1948, March 15). Across the Dial - Godfrey Tops Three First Places. *Akron Beacon Journal.*, p. 19.

Offineer, B. (1947, October 30). Alan Freed Airs From Jay Teen. *Akron Beacon Journal.*, p. 53.

Offineer, D. (1946, January 16).Around the Dial - Freed Sings and Fans Write. *Akron Beacon Journal.*, p. 4.

Offineer, B. (1947, April 25). Around the Dial - Spelling Bee Finals Air Tonight. *Akron Beacon Journal.*, p. 18.

Offineer, B. (1948, July 19). Around the Dial - Two New Shows Start Tonight. *Akron Beacon Journal.*, p. 11.

Offineer, B. (1947, June 29.) Around the Dial – Whiteman Joins Disc Spinners. *Akron Beacon Journal.*, p. 7-B.

OK Permit for Another Moon Dog Ball. (1952, May 13). *Akron Beacon Journal.*

"Payola" Probes Bring Wave of Resignations. (1959, November 24). *Journal Herald.*, p. 1.

Pete Myers Dies of Shotgun Blast. (October 5, 1968.) *New York Times.* p. 35

Pete Myers – DJ "Mad Daddy". Retrieved March 4, 2008 from http://www.recordsbymail.com/madDaddy.php

Pete Myers, Ex-Disc Jockey Here, Is Dead. (October 5, 1968.) *Cleveland Press.* p. C1

Petkovic, John. (June 17, 2003.) Shock 'n' Roll – A new CD revives the jive of a Cleveland radio icon. *Plain Dealer.* p. E1 – E3

Petkovic, John. (February 7, 2009.) The Trash Man – The Cramps' Lux Interior pioneered a whole new culture of rock. *Plain Dealer.* p. E1

Pioneer in Rock 'n' Roll to Face Quiz in Payola. (1959, November 23). *News-Messenger.*, p. 1.

"Presley Return Sparks Wide Air Activity." (1960, March 7). *The Billboard*, 1.

"Program Upheaval Spurs Jazz Spins." (1960, April 11). *The Billboard*, 19.

Programming a Giant. (1967, April 8). *Billboard*, *79*(14), 38.

Programming Panel. (1961, July 3). *Billboard*, *73*(26), 10.

"Promo Man Joins DJs Waxing as Pop Artists." (1962, March 3). *Billboard*, 26.

Radio Response Rating. (1965, August 14). *Billboard*, *77*(33), 54.

Reviews of new singles. (1962 November 3). *Billboard*, 20.

Rock 'n' Roll Fans in 23 States Join Society. (1975, July 21). *News Journal.*, p. 25.

Rolontz, B. (1963, January 26). "The 'First Family' Story - Wow!" *Billboard*, *75*(4), 6.

Rubin, Herbert J. & Rubin, Irene. (1995.) *Qualitative Interviewing: The Art of Hearing Data*. Thousand Oaks, California: Sage Publications, Inc.

Schoenherr, Steven E. (1999) Golden Age of Radio 1935-50. Retrieved February 20, 2007 from http://history.sandiego.edu/gen/recording/radio2.html

Scott., J. (1968, May 3). Early rockers make our scene. *Plain Dealer PD Action Tab.*, p. 2.

Scott, J., & Comer, C. (1959, January 24). Echoes from Kennard. *Call & Post.*, p. 7B.

Shippy., D. (1959, August 2). Keep Off the Suede Shoes. *Akron Beacon Journal.*, p. 4.

Shippy., D. (1963., May 19). Dick Shippy's Mailbag. *Akron Beacon Journal.*, p. 9F.

Shippy., D. (1959, August 2). Keep Off the Suede Shoes. *Akron Beacon Journal.*, p. 4D.

Shippy., D. (1959, July 21). 'Mad Daddy' Muzzled. *Akron Beacon Journal.*, p. 14.

Shippy., D. (1959, July 24). The Radio-TV Mailbag - Kids Need Paddles, Not Channels. *Akron Beacon Journal.*, p. 22.

Something to Remember. (1968, May 10). *Plain Dealer.*, p. 30.

Spitz, B. (2006). *The Beatles: The Biography.* Aurum. P. 170

Stakes, Damon. (1995.) *Cleveland Rocks: A Bicentennial Political and Social History of Cleveland 1796-1996.* (Shaker Heights, Ohio: York Publishing Company.)

Stewart., D. L. (1985, October 13). Cleveland Sound? Let's Recognize the City's Role in Rock. *Dayton Daily News.*, pp. 1-H.

Stutz, Marie R. (2002.) Thank Goodness for Cleveland Radio! Retrieved February 19, 2007 from http://moderncleveland.com/radio.

Suit Trips Freed's Kilocycle Hop. (1950, February 18). *Salem News.*

Summary of Major News. (October 4, 1968) *New York Times.*

The Mad Daddy Wavy Gravy ! Atom Smashin' Zoomeratin' Mello Jello Radio Broadcasts 1958-64 (Norton Records, 2003.) (December 14, 1949.)

The Mintz behind rock "n" roll myth. Cleveland.com. (2011, January 18). https://www.cleveland.com/pdextra/2011/01/the_mintz_behind_rock_n_roll_m.html

Thurber, J. (1999, September 19). Louis Hardin; New York Musical Moondog. *Los Angeles Times.*

Trattner, D. (2007, March 27). *Schoolhouse Rock.* Cleveland Magazine. https://clevelandmagazine.com/in-the-cle/commentary/articles/schoolhouse-rock

Travis, Carolyn & Gillson, Chris. (2008.) The Rise & Fall of Rock and Roll Radio. (Travisty Productions.)

Tull, Thomas B. (Ed.) (1947.) More Power To You. *this is ... WGAR – Going Forward With Radio.*

Tyler, K. (1964, September 1). What's Your Problem? *Newsday.*, pp. 11 C.

Van Tassel, David D. & Grabowski, John J. (1996). *The Dictionary of Cleveland Biography.* Bloomington & Indianapolis, Indiana: Indiana University Press.

Van Tassel, David D. & Grabowski, John J. (1987). *The Encyclopedia of Cleveland History*. Bloomington & Indianapolis, Indiana: Indiana University Press.

Vox Jox. (1963, March 2). *Billboard, 75*(9), 55.

Wallechinsky, David. (1995.) *The People's Almanac presents the 20*[th] *Century*. Boston: Little, Brown and Company.

Watson, Elena M. (1991.) *Television Movie Horror Hosts*. Jefferson, N.C.: McFarland & Co.

Wavy Gravy and Mello Jello – The "Mad Daddy" Pete Myers Biography. Retrieved October 13, 2008 from http://www.freewebs.com/maddaddy/newyork.htm.

Wertheim, Arthur Frank. (1979.) *Radio Comedy*. New York: Oxford University Press.

"Western Deejays Hook on at WINS." (1962c, September 15). *Billboard, 74*(37), 26.

Whetmore, Edd. (1979.) *Mediamerica*. New York; Wadsworth, Inc.

White, C. W. (2016). The payola trial - the history of Boston Rock & Roll - Chapter 5 - features - motherlode.tv. https://www.motherlode.tv/bostonrock/chapter5.html

Whiteside, Jonny. (July 17, 2003.) Mad Daddy – DJ from Mars. Retrieved September 10, 2006 from http://www.laweekly.com/music/music/mad-daddy/2592/

Wilson, E. (1957, April 13). "Alan Freed, Rock and Roll Exponent", Boosting Rock-a-Billy in Gotham.". *Cleveland Plain Dealer*, p. 19.

WHK-AM Pete "Mad Daddy" Myers Show. (June 25, 1959.)

WHK-AM Pete "Mad Daddy" Myers Show. (October 15, 1958.)

WHK-AM Pete "Mad Daddy" Myers Show. (November 4, 1958.)

WHK Weekly Log. (November 23, 1929.) Vol.1, No. 4.

WINS-AM Pete "Mad Daddy" Myers Show. (May 5, 1963.)

WINS-AM Pete "Mad Daddy" Myers Show. (August 28, 1964.)

WJW-AM. (1952, April 7). Radio Alone Pulled 25,000! *Broadcasting Magazine*.

WJW's Freed Packs Em In! (1952, April 28). *Broadcasting Magazine*.

WJW's Pete Myers is Actor in Disguise. (January 31, 1958.) *Cleveland Press.*

WNEW Announcer Kills Self with Gun. (1968, October 5). *Newsday.*, p. 11.

"WNEW Fans Dig Dignity; 'Mad Daddy' Got 'Em Mad. (July 13, 1959.) *Billboard*

"WNEW Hikes Program Spans." (1960, July 25). *The Billboard*, 2.

"WNEW Jocks Answer the Big "Have You Ever?"". (1959, November 16). *The Billboard*, 16.

WXEN-FM Pete "Mad Daddy" Myers Memorial Show. (October, 1968.) Hosted by Harry Hinz.

WZAK-FM Dick Liberatore "Big Beat Show." (1967.) featuring the interview with Pete "Mad Daddy" Myers.

Appendix

Billy Bass, personal communication, April 10, 2021.

Jay Hunt, personal communication, January 25, 2009.

Jim Jaworski, personal communication, February 22, 2007.

Rich Klein, personal communication, August 29, 2021.

Jim LaBarbara, personal communication, August 6, 2021.

Neil McIntyre, personal communication, November 8, 2006.

Greg Miller, personal communication, February 22, 2007.

Ernie Myers, personal communication, October 4, 2006.

Steve Nemeth, personal communication, May 19, 2021.

Norm N. Nite, personal communication, January 24, 2007.

Tom Pope, personal communication, January 22, 2021.

Carl Reese, personal communication, March 2011.

Walter Sabo, personal communication, July 2016.

About the Authors

Mike Olszewski is a veteran radio *I* TV *I* print journalist and author with a long history of teaching college-level communications and journalism courses. He holds masters' degrees in journalism & mass communications and an MLIS with an emphasis on museum work and archiving. Best known for his work at the legendary WMMS-FM, Mike has devoted his life to historical research documenting media and pop culture. Along with his written work he has also won acclaim for his TV and radio documentaries, and a segment of his book *Radio Daze* was adapted for the stage at the prestigious Cleveland Playhouse.

Janice Olszewski is a careful and dedicated researcher who, along with her husband, is a frequent guest at libraries and conventions discussing their books on media and how it shaped and reflected the times we live in. Her work has appeared in national magazines including *Filmfax, Outre*, and others.

Leo Mintz' Record Rendezvous was an innovator in marketing new releases. (Cleveland Memory Project / Michael Schwartz Library)

With listening booths and direct access to new releases, Record Rendezvous became a "must visit" stop for shoppers in downtown Cleveland. (Cleveland Memory Project / Michael Schwartz Library)

Mintz' Record Rendezvous introduced direct access to records for shoppers visiting his store. (Cleveland Memory Project / Michael Schwartz Library)

Leo Mintz could look back on a worldwide phenomena that he not only helped create but also popularized its name. (Cleveland Memory Project / Michael Schwartz Library)

Alan Freed was among the pioneers in Cleveland Television at WXEL-TV, but necessarily by choice. (Author's Collection)

Alan Freed and his family enjoyed a very comfortable life at their home in Connecticut, though some questioned how he funded that lifestyle. (Author's Collection)

Alan Freed at the height of his popularity at WJW / Cleveland. (CPL/ Photograph Collection)

Notice that this ticket to the infamous Moondog Ball does not designate the first or second show. (Trattner Family collection)

WJW's Virg Brinnon tried, but how do you follow an act like Alan Freed? (Author's Collection)

Brinnon's fan club cards stressed *The Moondog House* to call back to its original host. (Author's Collection)

Named the "Top Jock" in the United States by *Time* magazine, WERE's Bill Randle had a tight rein on new acts hoping to get his blessing. (CPL/Photograph Collection)

Stressing his "loveable, laughable" presence, WJW's Pete Myers was a far cry from the Mad Daddy personae he would assume in the evening hours. (CPL/Photograph Collection)

Mad Daddy is seen with WJW continuity director Madeline Swim in a series of publicity photos seen as controversial even for the 1950s. (Author's Collection)

(Author's Collection)

(Author's Collection)

WJW's mobile air studio was seen as state of the art for its time and brought Myers' Mad Daddy to the public. (Cleveland Memory Project / Michael Schwartz Library)

Mad Daddy's publicity photo for WXEL-TV's *Shock Theater*.

Pete Myers poses outside the plane that would carry Mad Daddy in his legendary publicity jump over the treacherous waters of Lake Erie.

WHK wanted the public to know that Mad Daddy had found a new home farther down the radio dial. (Author's Collection)

WHK's official promotional photo upon Pete Myers' arrival. (CPL/ Photograph Collection)

Former WHK personality Ernie Anderson worked with Myers and would later adapt some of his sayings when he became WJW-TV's "Ghoulardi". (Cleveland Memory Project / Michael Schwartz Library)

Ernie Anderson's "Ghoulardi" took Cleveland by storm on WJW-TV after his time working with Pete Myers. (Cleveland Memory Project / Michael Schwartz Library)

Bill "Smoochie" Gordon was a ratings magnet at WHK, WERE and other stations. He signed off is show with his trademark, "Stay Smoochie, you rascal you!" (Cleveland Memory Project / Michael Schwartz Library)

WNEW's Pete Myers was reunited with WIXY's Joe Finan at the Mad Daddy's final appearance at the Cleveland Arena. (CPL/Photograph Collection)

Alan Freed had a day in court with the original "Moondog", New York street artist Louis Hardin, who used that title long before Freed adapted it for his radio show. (CPL/Photograph Collection)

Former WJW general manager William Lemmon was still working well into the 1970s. (CPL/Photograph Collection)

Despite fingers pointed in his direction, Dick Clark remained one of the prime movers of popular music with *American Bandstand*. He's seen here with Freddy "Boom Boom" Cannon (CPL/Photograph Collection)

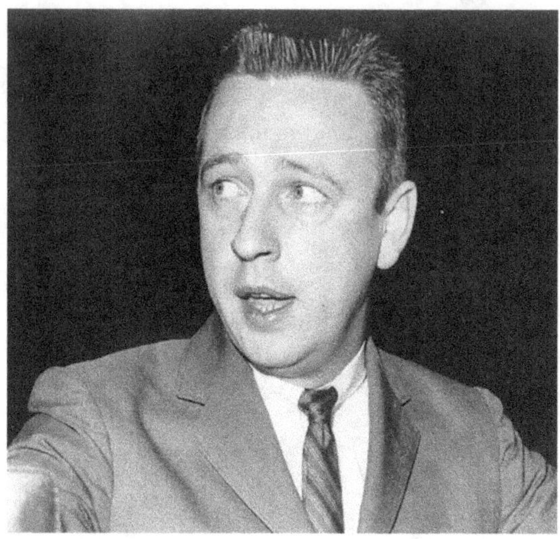

Years after refusing to cooperate in the payola hearings, Joe Finan returned to Cleveland radio and what would be a final reunion with his friend, Pete Myers. (CPL/Photograph Collection)

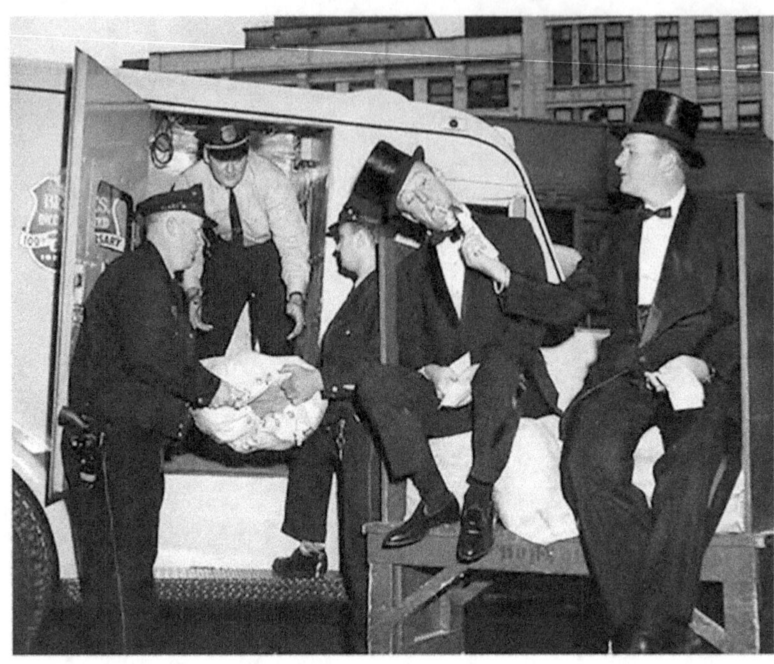

Myers long time friend Joe Finan gets a light from fellow Cleveland radio personality Big Wilson.

KYW's Joe Finan, attorney Don Zimmerman and fellow KYW disc jockey Wes Hopkins wait to testify at the payola hearings.

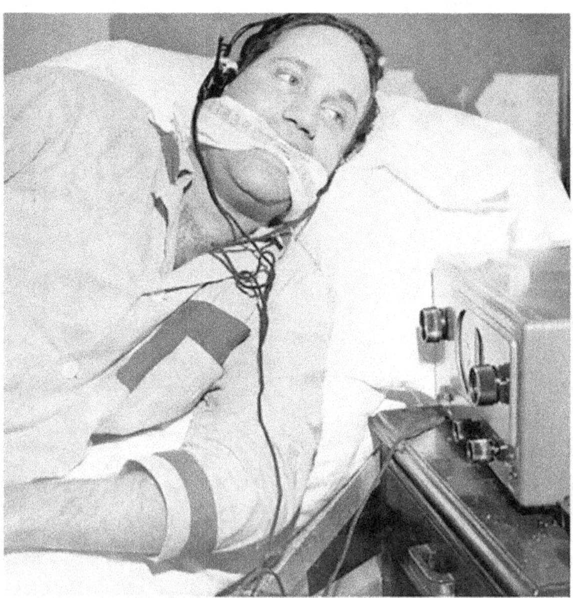

Many a program director thought this was the only way to control
WHK's Bill Gordon.

Mad Daddy on TV! – WJW-TV offered Myers a chance to host its
late-night horror show. He was frustrated that the heavy TV cameras
couldn't be attached to the ceiling so he would appear upside down.

Caption: Mad Daddy made a series of appearances at Northeast Ohio theaters promising a visit from "It" on stage.